"Linda Talley is not only just a great coach, but a creative communicator who teaches us the fine art of communicating for just-the-right effect in tough situations. Miss reading this book and you will miss opportunities to relate so much better with people."

Ray Anthony, author of *Talking to the Top*

"Linda Talley has truly mastered Business Finesse--Dealing With Sticky Situations in the Workplace for Managers! She has taken the most difficult situations regarding poor communication and 'lack of language' and solved them with an easy to use, results oriented process, that when the initiative is taken to practice and use, simply cannot fail."

Harrison Fisher, Regional Sales Manager,
Vice President, Chase Manhattan Bank

"Management used to be a jungle. Today it's a swamp. Just as many visible dangers, with the added challenge of navigating through unseen bogs, unexpected pits, and thinly camouflaged pools of quicksand. Linda Talley's book is a map through that swamp. . .and more. She not only shows us a safe pathway, she also tells us what to do if we stray from that path."

John J. McGrath, Ph.D., Director,
Marketing & Management Communication,
Argonne National Laboratory

"Linda's three steps help professionals reach an understanding of business finesse, communicating effectively on a spiritual level."

Jean DeWitt, Ph.D.,
Coordinator of Speech Communication,
University of Houston--Downtown

"This is the best reference book on actual business situations that I have ever seen. It offers exactly what business people need to be successful--language."

Mike McAdams, Owner,
Lake Austin Spa Resort

"Linda is tuning us into the 'Age of Consciousness' by helping us understand an awareness that people are achieving about the spirit power of personal truth and mutual respect. If we are to succeed in our relationships with others, Linda's guidelines for questioning for greater understanding and then telling our truth can be the beginning to establishing the trusting relationships with people we all desire and want."

Joseph P. Sasso, Futurist, President,
Team 2 LEarn

"Crisp, user friendly and insightful. You will find application of these tools for both work and home."

G. Eric Allenbaugh, Ph.D.,
Author of *Wake Up Calls*

Business Finesse

Dealing With Sticky Situations in the Workplace for Managers

Linda Talley

Leadership U Press

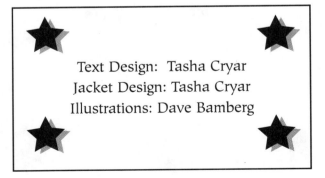

Text Design: Tasha Cryar
Jacket Design: Tasha Cryar
Illustrations: Dave Bamberg

To my friends and family, who love me, care for me and support me.

Thanks...

Numerous thanks are in order to people who have helped me develop and refine the Business Finesse concept and, also, this book.

First, to Ben Whitley, who has stood by me through every part of this book and has read it more times than I.

To Dave Bamberg, whose creative illustrative genius, has touched my life and the lives of my audiences.

To Ray Anthony who believed in me and knew this book was possible even when I gave up.

To Tasha Cryar who has made my manuscript look like a book.

To Marie Robinson for trying and succeeding with Business Finesse.

To Kevin Dawes, Kim White, Kathy Fishelberg, Kirk Hellofs, Pat Shaw, David Antczak, Colleen Richardson who have given me situations which are included in this book.

To numerous other people who have given me situations but not their names.

To all the meeting planners who have let me share my idea of Business Finesse with their audiences.

To Nancy Vogel, my sister, my computer guru, my friend, who is forever at my side.

And to my mother, Betty Vogel, who made this all possible!

Thank you all for everything. Thank you for going the extra mile for me.

About The Author

Linda Talley is a popular keynote speaker and corporate consultant. She is known as the "How-to" Coach and is a nationally recognized speaker who speaks on personal leadership, change and advanced communication skills.

Her first book, **Business Finesse: How to Say the Right Thing at the Right Time**, is a handbook of specific language for situations consultants face in their daily business. Readers have said they keep this book on the desk as a reference manual.

She is the President of Leadership University, an executive development firm located in Houston, Texas. She founded Leadership University as a way to develop more and better leaders who can meet the ever increasing demands of the global marketplace and the rapid pace of change in the information age. Her programs provide new awareness and information that enable people to take the leadership role in all areas of business as well as in their personal life. Linda believes that organizations of all sizes will look to leaders at all levels within the organization in order to move into the 21st century.

Linda received her bachelor's degree from the University of Texas at Austin and her master's degree from Central Michigan University.

Table of Contents

Preface

Language--Using the right words at the right time.

Different language offers dramatically different results. How you use language and the language you use is a direct function of you knowing yourself, trusting yourself and being able to access your power. It's truly the difference between knowing what you need and knowing what you want and being able to articulate the difference.

For most, the steps and language in this book will act as a stepping stone to get you on your path to getting what you want out of each business situation. Even if you don't get it all, you'll get a lot more than someone who doesn't use the steps and language in this book. It's like one of my software programs. It comes with a wizard for newsletters. I didn't do a newsletter for several years because I didn't know how to "lay it out" even though I had the wizard. I was afraid. As I grew personally and professionally, I said to myself one day: "I have this wizard. Why not try it?" I tried it, and even though the first newsletter wasn't perfect, each time I did it, it got better. Now newsletters are a piece of cake. The same is true for the steps and the language in this book. Use the language till you can make up your own. It will be a habit before you know it. Habits come from doing something over and over again. Use these steps and the language until they become a habit. Can you imagine making a habit out of knowing exactly what to say in key business situations? It's been said that it takes thirty days to install a new habit. Any new habit takes time.

Helplessness and mastery are both habits. So is Business Finesse. They are all habits that we have learned. Which ones do you want to keep?

Introduction

My first book, **Business Finesse: How to Say the Right Thing at the Right Time**, was written to give my clients specific language for specific situations. Many of my clients were upset because they wanted something out of a business situation and didn't get it. So they came to me and wanted to know what they could have said or done differently in order to get what they wanted. I gave them the language but it was only language and not a process. I gave them fish but I didn't teach them how to fish.

I wrote the second book to share my depth of knowledge rather than my ability as a wordsmith. Here I'm teaching people how to fish so they can feed themselves forever and communicate effectively in every business situation. This book showcases my essence. It showcases what I really do: show people how to build relationships, become more productive and profitable through communication.

I'm a process expert. I take you from theory to implementation. After you've read Tom Peters and Stephen Covey, you're ready to implement. This book gives you a three step process and the language for fifty business situations so you can say what you really want to say in any business situation. Any sort of implementation needs a process and it needs language.

Linguistics experts estimate that the average citizen's vocabulary is decreasing by roughly 1% a year. The English language has more than 450,000 words. More than 80% of our daily conversations are made up of a mere 400 words--of which the most commonly used are "me, my, I, mine."

Words have been the building blocks of our society, of our businesses. We have lots of words but we don't know how to put them together in a way that creates what we want. In other words, we don't use words effectively. Words and the way we put them together, language, are how we're going to get exactly what we want.

Historically, we have used words to seduce, manipulate, alienate or coerce people into doing what we wanted them to do. Now you can use words in the right order and at the right time to get exactly what you want by having language that says the right thing at the right time. In today's world, language has power. Use language to ask for what you want and to say everything. It has more power and it's healthier than seduction, manipulation, alienation or coercion.

Business Finesse is a skill to use language to achieve better relationships, increased productivity and profitability. "To language" is a skill that you master in order to be able to articulate what you feel, need, want. It's using words in the right order and at the right time. It comes from the heart, so there is no emotion or ego attached. It's simply what you feel, need or want. You can use clichés or jargon, but when you language, you come from your heart, and people can then truly hear what you have to say. Someone can talk a lot and be very verbose without actually saying a lot.

The key is to say what really matters and say it in a fashion which the other person can understand. When people can understand you, they can relate to you. When they can relate to you, you form relationships with them, and when you form relationships with them, you achieve results. We all want results, but results come from relationships. Not the other way around. This book will help you develop a systematic approach to communicating effectively and gives you the language you need to form the relationships that you really want in order to achieve bigger and better results.

Part 1
Chapter 1
Why Communication Fails

"Don't focus on building up your weaknesses.
Understand your strengths and place yourself in a
position where these strengths count. Your strengths
are what will carry you through to success."

Peter Drucker

Many people have told me that they know how to communicate effectively. Now, I'm not a therapist but I call that delusional thinking. Nine times out of ten, we fail to communicate because we don't have the language to ask for what we really need, first, and want, second. We don't have the language to say all that needs to be said to our internal and external clients.

Remember the communication model you learned back in elementary school where you had the sender and the receiver? The sender was the one who sent the message and the receiver was the one who heard the message. The story I was told was that if the sender sent the message and the receiver heard the message, everything would be all right. As I've worked in the business arena, I now realize that is not true! The sender may send the message but the receiver doesn't usually hear the message exactly as it is sent. It goes through all kinds of filters from the sender to the receiver before it is actually heard by the receiver. While it moves through filters, such as your belief systems, myths, what your mother said you should do, etc., the message gets changed. What usually happens is that the receiver amplifies or magnifies what is pleasing or positive and blocks out what is not.

During programs that I have presented to associations and corporations, I have conducted research on the outcome of messages sent between a sender and receiver. In order to add the filters, I play the game we used to play in grade school where you start a message at the front of the room and the last person at the back of the room to receive it repeats what he or she heard. Usually it is nothing close to the original message. Back in grade school, usually elementary school, this was considered child's play. However, it had a very strong message that I didn't hear back then and today I teach it: Effective Communication is more than just spoken words. When I have given a message to a group to whom I am speaking and have asked them to pass the message along, it never comes out right--regardless of whether the message is positive or negative. We seem to block out so much during the communication process. When we block out so much, we miss a lot.

When we miss a lot during the communication process, several things happen. First of all, relationships are diminished. After awhile, they become stifled and boring. Second, our productivity is decreased. When we have to say more than necessary--or go back to re-do work because something wasn't communicated properly--effectiveness and efficiency are greatly reduced. Third, profitability decreases. If you are not building great relationships and you are not being effective, you are going to have a tough time being profitable. And even if you are profitable, it will be at great emotional and physical expense. The quality of your relationships is directly related to your ability to communicate effectively. Your productivity and profitability are directly related to your ability to communicate effectively. It could be said that communication is the most important aspect of successful relationships, productivity and profitability. The question is: how to sustain all three?

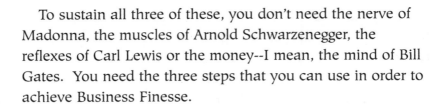

To sustain all three of these, you don't need the nerve of Madonna, the muscles of Arnold Schwarzenegger, the reflexes of Carl Lewis or the money--I mean, the mind of Bill Gates. You need the three steps that you can use in order to achieve Business Finesse.

Think about this:

Communication fails because:

1. You don't have the language you need to ask for what you want or say all that needs to be said.
2. You amplify what is pleasing and block out what is not.
3. You maintain belief systems that are no longer true and no longer serve you.

4

Part 1

Chapter 2

The Definition of Business Finesse

"Those who won't, project,
Those who can't, seduce,
Those who do, use Business Finesse."

Linda Talley

My first book on the subject, **Business Finesse: How to Say the Right Thing at the Right Time**, was reviewed by Joyce Lain Kennedy, a nationally syndicated columnist. She said that Business Finesse was personalizing business in the workplace. Until she wrote that, I had not really defined Business Finesse. After she wrote it and after I thought about it, I decided that that wasn't really my definition of Business Finesse. Now, don't get me wrong. I did not send her a letter and tell her that she was wrong. What I did do was send her a letter and thank her because she helped me get a lot of visibility for the book. As a result, I sold many copies.

The first book was more of me being a wordsmith. The book included 100 business situations and the language to use to get what you wanted out of each situation. My coaching clients had been asking for the book and so I wrote it. However, I have now developed my own definition of Business Finesse. But before I tell you, let me first tell you how I came to the definition I use.

When I first begin to think about the definition for the model of Business Finesse, I thought that it might be an art form. You hear those words tossed around all the time and it sounded good to me. However, when I gave it some thought, I realized that the art that I like is not the art that some of my friends like. Many people enjoy a Picasso. I prefer Monet. Your art form may not be my art form, so Business Finesse, as an art form, might not fit with what other people enjoy. So the word "art" seemed to be a deterrent.

Then I thought about using the word "science," because I come from a scientific background and this is a model I have developed. After giving that word some thought, I decided against it because of my older sister. She was told by her high school guidance counselor that she would never achieve in the realm of science or math and that she should seek a liberal arts degree. She did and to this day, she can't balance a check book. So my fear was that if I called it a science, I would scare a lot of people away from the book. I needed something that was people friendly. Something that would attract people to my book.

One day as I was sitting at my computer and contemplating my computer screen saver, the idea hit me as soon as the words appeared in my head. The word "skill" appeared in my mind and I said, "that's it!" A skill is something anyone can learn and use, if they really want to and if they are ready and if they are able. So right then and there, I decided that Business Finesse is the skill of communicating effectively in the workplace so that you can achieve three goals: great relationships, increased productivity and increased profitability.

Great relationships, increased productivity and profitability--that's great, but how does Business Finesse fit into the communication process? Here's how!

We communicate at two different levels. The first level is the emotional level. This is where most of us communicate on a daily basis. At this level, you are communicating from

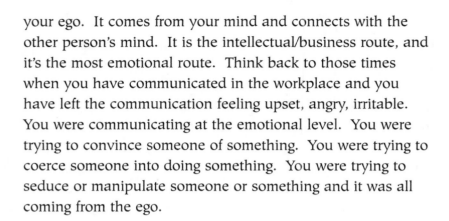

your ego. It comes from your mind and connects with the other person's mind. It is the intellectual/business route, and it's the most emotional route. Think back to those times when you have communicated in the workplace and you have left the communication feeling upset, angry, irritable. You were communicating at the emotional level. You were trying to convince someone of something. You were trying to coerce someone into doing something. You were trying to seduce or manipulate someone or something and it was all coming from the ego.

It's the ego that causes those feelings because the ego is that part of you which thinks things and people should be a certain way, rather than the way they really are. So the ego is the perfect device for making people and even yourself wrong. I'll tell you later on what happens when you make someone wrong or when you are made wrong. When the ego is involved in communicating, more than likely it will be a failed communication. The ego must be eliminated. Keep in mind that the ego is not to be tossed aside lightly. It won't go that way.

Eliminating the ego is a daily task. It sneaks back into your life through the back door to create stress and drama and upset and because it came in through the back door, you don't even know it's there. You wonder why you are reacting or feeling this way. Now you know. Whenever you feel upset, concerned, stressed out, ask yourself, "Is this really me or is this the ego?" More often than not it's the ego. Eliminate it with force!

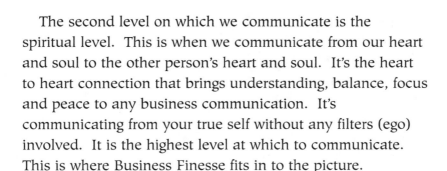

The second level on which we communicate is the spiritual level. This is when we communicate from our heart and soul to the other person's heart and soul. It's the heart to heart connection that brings understanding, balance, focus and peace to any business communication. It's communicating from your true self without any filters (ego) involved. It is the highest level at which to communicate. This is where Business Finesse fits in to the picture.

When you use the skill of Business Finesse, you are eliminating the ego and coming from your heart in order to touch the other person's heart. It's usually done in a gentle and caring way. In fact, keep in mind that communication is not loud, fantastic or grand. Communication is when you touch the heart of the other person in the most loving and caring and attentive way, and you can do that when you use Business Finesse.

Let me give you a personal example of these two levels of communication. Last year I was traveling to a convention in Orlando. On the final approach to the Orlando airport, as the flight attendant was telling us to put our seats and tray tables in their upright and locked position, I remembered that I had forgotten to pack my little black satin shoes for the gala at the conclusion of the convention. After the first thought of pure panic, I sat back in my seat and said, "No sweat. I'll have Page, my next door neighbor, get my shoes and 'express mail' them to me." I was completely confident because this was Saturday, and I didn't need them till Tuesday.

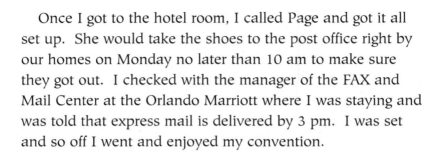

Once I got to the hotel room, I called Page and got it all set up. She would take the shoes to the post office right by our homes on Monday no later than 10 am to make sure they got out. I checked with the manager of the FAX and Mail Center at the Orlando Marriott where I was staying and was told that express mail is delivered by 3 pm. I was set and so off I went and enjoyed my convention.

On Tuesday at 3:15 pm, I checked with the Manager at the FAX and Mail Center. She went behind a door and came out and told me that there was no package for me. I thanked her for looking and then asked her if I could ask her something else. She said "Yes." So I said that the box had to be there because I had to have this package and would she please check one more time. She did and came back empty handed. Of course, I was beside myself because I had not used Federal Express. I felt sick inside because I had trusted the post office again, and again, they didn't deliver my mail.

The Manager asked me who sent the package and I told her it was the post office. She said that I should call and find out what happened. She dialed the number of the post office in Houston for me (yes, I keep the post office's number because I have had that many problems with them). I told the postal employee who answered the phone what the problem was and she told me that if I didn't have the number of the original receipt they couldn't track it. She hung up on me. I was angry. I then tried to call Page to get the receipt number but she wasn't home. So in disgust, I

told the Manager that "I guess Cinderella isn't going to go to the ball tonight."

Now, let me stop for a minute. The way the postal employee and I had communicated was at the emotional level. She hung up on me and if it were possible, I probably would have flown back to Houston in that instant and strangled her even though I didn't know her name. If they treat an external customer the way they treated me, can you imagine how they treat their internal customers? Pretty scary! The postal employee and I were both very emotional and it was all ego. But let me tell you what happened next.

The Manager said, "You feel pretty sad because you didn't get your box, and you can't go to the party, right?"
I said, "Yes."
She said, "Are you willing to stick around here for awhile with me?"
I said, "Yes."
She said, "Good, because Cinderella is going to the ball!"

She got back on the phone and called her local post office. She talked with someone and told them what the situation was and wrote down an 800 number. Then she dialed the 800 number and told someone what the situation was and wrote down several more numbers. She called one of those numbers and said, "I believe you have a box there that we need. We have Mrs. Hillary Clinton staying with us and you have a box she needs for tonight. Will you check to make sure it's there?"

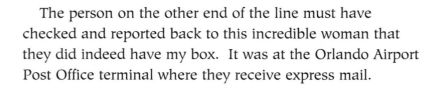

The person on the other end of the line must have checked and reported back to this incredible woman that they did indeed have my box. It was at the Orlando Airport Post Office terminal where they receive express mail.

The Manager then said, "I need that box for my guest. Will you deliver it to me this afternoon?"
She obviously received a positive answer because she hung up the phone, turned to me and said, "Now, Ms. Talley, you go up to your room, take a nap and your box will be here shortly. I'll call you as soon as it arrives."

I had tears in my eyes. This woman had touched my heart. She really cared about me and my shoes. She spent her dime and her time to take care of me and be concerned about me and I could feel it.

I thanked her and went up to my room. It was approximately 4:30 pm when I left her area.

At 5:50 pm, I received a call from the front desk (the gala starts at 6:30). They have a package for me. I rush downstairs and there is my shoe box. A little crushed, a little bruised, but there are my shoes. I grab the box, thank them and rush around to the FAX and Mail Center. There's my Manager. I show her the shoe box and say, "I couldn't have done it without you. I guess Cinderella is going to the ball."

And I did go to the ball. But the reason I went to the ball was because this Manager communicated with me and the postal employees at the spiritual level. I doubt that she has ever heard of Business Finesse, but she used the skill quite well that day and created miracles for me. She touched my heart in the most loving, caring and attentive way. And I could feel it. She communicated with me and the postal employees in a way that got results--got action! And she did it by building relationships. She didn't communicate at the emotional level. She was way above that!

I read somewhere in a book and copied down what Carl Jung had once written in a commentary on the Chinese document, *The Secret of the Golden Flower,* "I have often seen individuals simply outgrow a problem which had destroyed others. This 'outgrowing' was seen to consist in a new level of consciousness. Some higher or wider interest arose in the person's horizon, and through this widening of his view the insoluble problem lost its urgency. It was not solved logically but faded out when confronted with a new and stronger life tendency. It was not repressed and made unconscious, but merely appeared in a different light, and so did indeed become different. What, on a lower level, had led to the wildest conflicts and to panicky outbursts of emotion, viewed from the higher level of the personality, now seemed like a storm in the valley seen from a high mountain-top. This does not mean that the thunderstorm is robbed of its reality, but instead of being in it, one is above it."

To me, this explains communicating at the spiritual level rather than the emotional level. When I read this, I just said, "Yes! I know what he means." I know what he's talking

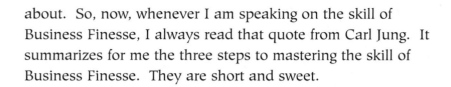

about. So, now, whenever I am speaking on the skill of Business Finesse, I always read that quote from Carl Jung. It summarizes for me the three steps to mastering the skill of Business Finesse. They are short and sweet.

The three steps of Business Finesse are:
Step #1. Make people right.
Step #2. Ask permission.
Step #3. Tell the truth.

By using these three steps, you create the realm of possibility and the space to have a conversation with another and get what you want. The challenge is that most of us attempt to get what we want through verbal force, threat, power, coercion and it just doesn't work. When you attempt to force your opinion on someone else, they retreat or move backwards or react because they feel they are being treated as something less than human. We do this because we have trained ourselves to do it. We think people want our advice, opinion, knowledge or ideas. They may want it but we must condition the conversation and give it context in order for them to hear the advice or information. Giving advice, information, knowledge or your opinion occurs at Step 3 in the process of Business Finesse. There are two critically important steps before Step 3 that most of us overlook. Unfortunately we rush in and we usually create conflict rather than relationships.

Relationships do not grow in an environment where we force our opinions on others or give them more information than they want. By using the three steps of Business Finesse, you will enable the person you are communicating with to respond out of choice rather than react to a perceived threat.

Three steps--that's all. When I teach people these three steps, some say, "that was so easy. It's so basic." Yes, it is. It's so easy, it's almost silly. Marie Robinson, a credit executive with a spice and extract manufacturer, attended one of my programs on Business Finesse and wrote to me, "I have tried it on three difficult co-workers and got very positive results. Can you believe that? Before the class I could argue, fuss and turn blue and these people would not be phased. The three steps worked on these three people and if they worked on them--IT WORKS!"

In 1759, Samuel Butler added "learned" to nonsense to come up with the saying "learned nonsense." I just loved that saying when I read it. And it immediately occurred to me that is what Business Finesse is. Butler said "for learned nonsense has a deeper sound than easy sense, and goes far more profound." Business Finesse is learned nonsense. It's basic and it appears logical but only after you think about it for awhile and then laugh. Business Finesse or "Learned Nonsense" works to make communication a pleasure and keeps that process going. Thank you Mr. Butler.

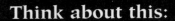

Think about this:

Business Finesse is a skill that you can develop in order to achieve long-term relationships, increased productivity and higher profitability.

Business Finesse is a three-step process:

Step #1. Make people right.

Step #2. Ask permission.

Step #3. Tell the truth.

Part 1

Chapter 3

Step One: Make People Right!

"Everything that happens, when it has significance, is in the nature of a contradiction."

Henry Miller

Step One: Make People Right!

Why? Because they are right for their level of development at that particular time and space in their life.

When you come from the notion that people are right, you accept them just as they are without any conditions attached. Consider the statement: "You are perfect just the way you are. I would not change a thing about you." Feel those words touch your heart. Can you hear yourself saying to yourself, "I wish someone would say that to me right now!" Even if someone did walk right up to you this very minute and say those words to you, it would be a very different experience. For most of us, that would feel very unusual because we are conditioned to be accepted--with conditions attached.

When you make people wrong, you accept them with conditions attached and we are much more used to that scenario. Consider the statement: "This would work much better if only you would do your own work." "You'd find a job if only you lost some weight." Sound familiar? It sounds familiar and it feels more comfortable because that's what you are used to hearing. That's what you are conditioned to hear from an early age. The major problem with this type of communication is that when you make people wrong, they won't move or grow towards you regardless of what other techniques you use. Why? Because they've been made wrong.

Every person has needs. Most of us have the need to be accepted, approved of, appreciated, valued, made to feel special. When we make people right, we help them get these needs met. And when we help them get these needs met, we build a relationship with them. When we build a relationship with them, we can then achieve other goals such as higher productivity and profitability. However, if you don't have a relationship first, it will be difficult to achieve these last two goals. Results come from relationships--not the other way around.

When we make people wrong, we go up to them and voice a complaint directly to them rather than asking for what we need or want--a relationship with them. That person usually becomes silent, tries to change the subject or leaves the room or meeting. They have been made wrong and you have maintained the status quo--no relationship with them. Nothing has changed from that interaction. It's a lose-lose situation. When we make people wrong, we don't build relationships and we don't achieve the goals or results we want. Why? Because when we make people wrong, they put up there "shields."

Let me tell you about shields. If you haven't seen one of the television episodes or movies with Capt. Kirk and the starship, Enterprise, this may not mean as much to you. If you have seen an episode, you'll see exactly what I'm talking about.

Remember on one of those episodes when Capt. Kirk is sitting in his big console chair on the bridge and Mr. Spock has just informed him that there is a Romulan ship "out there," even though the crew and the rest of us can't see it. The way the story goes is that the Romulans can move around in space in their invisible, cloaked, format but they can be detected by the starship in that invisible format. Shortly after being informed about the Romulans, Capt. Kirk tells Mr. Sulu, "Shields up, Mr. Sulu."

You see Mr. Sulu push a button and you don't see anything happen, but you know that the shields are up. And then Mr. Sulu turns to Capt. Kirk and says, "Shields up, Sir!"

At the very next moment, you're looking out through the big viewing screen on the bridge. Suddenly the Romulan ship appears. Again, that's the story. It has to become visible in order to fire on the starship. And it does commence firing.

Capt. Kirk is trying to hold onto his chair, Mr. Spock is holding onto his portion of the console and poor Mr. Sulu falls out of his chair. Have you ever seen a Star Trek episode when the Enterprise is attacked and Mr. Sulu doesn't fall out of his chair?

Here's the question, this is supposed to happen in the 23rd century, right? I wonder what happened to OSHA? No seat belts, no air bags?

★ ★ ★ ★ ★ ★ ★ ★

At some point, Capt. Kirk instructs Mr. Sulu to fire on the Romulan vessel. And, of course, the Enterprise gets a direct hit and the Romulans are blown to "Kingdom Come."

Capt. Kirk then asks Mr. Spock for a casualty report and he replies, "No casualties."

He asks Mr. Scott for a damage report and Mr. Scott replies, "Minimal damage, Sir."

Do you know why? The shields were up and not much can get through when the shields are up.

The same is true for human beings. Unfortunately, humans don't have the ability, as the starship does, to raise and lower their shields on command. When you make someone wrong, their shields go up and it takes at least 24 to 48 hours for the shields to come down. It's an involuntary response. The person who has their shields up can't force the shields down. They have to come down when they come down and not a minute sooner.

Think of the member of your team, attending a Monday morning staff meeting. Someone in the room makes this person wrong. You even feel the sting of the "make wrong." After the meeting, this person doesn't walk, he runs back to his office and shuts the door. You haven't seen him for about three hours now and you want to take him to lunch. You knock on his door and you hear, "what do you want?" It is spoken in a very unfriendly voice. You're amazed

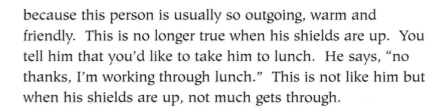

because this person is usually so outgoing, warm and friendly. This is no longer true when his shields are up. You tell him that you'd like to take him to lunch. He says, "no thanks, I'm working through lunch." This is not like him but when his shields are up, not much gets through.

When shields are up, relationships are diminished because you can't get through to the person. It's a protection measure for them just as it was for the starship, Enterprise.

Now, this person, who was made wrong, is usually a highly effective and efficient person. He usually has work to you in half the time as anyone else but these last two days, it's taken almost three times as long to get anything from him. Why? Because the shields are up and when the shields are up, productivity is decreased. His energy is going into keeping the shields up rather than getting his work done. Again, it's involuntary. He can't help but send energy to his shields rather than to his work.

Two days later, that same person comes into the office and tells you how tired he is and he can't figure it out because he has had eight hours of sleep every night this week. I'll tell you why he is tired. It's because he has had his shields up and when the shields are up, all his energy goes into keeping them up and when they finally do come down, the person is exhausted. He has used a tremendous amount of energy keeping the shields up. That's why they are so protective. It's a huge energy field.

You may have someone physically at the office but when the shields are up, emotionally they are not there. And guess what! Here's the bad news: Not only do you lose your employee for the two to three days that his or her shields are up, but you also lose productivity for two to three more days when they emotionally return to work because they are physically exhausted.

KEY INSIGHT: Next time you make one of your staff or associates wrong, be prepared to wait four to five days--if not longer, before they are up to speed again. Better yet, make them right and don't have any downtime.

The key to making people right is to get them to stand side-by-side with you as you move forward in the communication process. Making people right doesn't mean that you are surrendering to their will and way. You can make people right without losing anything in the conversation and by doing this, you create the realm of possibility for the conversation to move forward. Making people right does not mean agreeing with what they are saying (especially if it is wrong for you) but rather validating what they are saying.

The way to think about this is the way I demonstrate it in front of my audiences. I bring two "volunteers" up from the audience and have them stand back-to-back. One is facing the front of the room and one is facing the back of the room or towards the audience. Then I ask the person facing the front of the room to begin describing what she sees.

She might mention a projector, screen, a beige colored wall with molding half-way up, a double door with an exit sign over it. At this point, I usually stop her. I leave her facing forward and go to the person facing the audience and ask him what he sees. He usually says, "lots of smiling faces, about five hundred people sitting in chairs, two sets of double doors on the right and two sets of double doors on the left, a small door at the end of the room." At this point, I usually stop him. Then I ask the audience, "Who's right?" And before they can answer, I ask another question, "WHO CARES?" This always gets a laugh from the audience because WHO CARES?! If the person facing the front of the room is a client of the person facing the audience, who cares?!

I ask how the person facing the audience can make the person facing the front of the room right? What can he say? Here's what I suggest:

"I can see why you would say what you just said. Would you be willing to turn 180 degrees and look at things from my perspective?" The audience then agrees that this is good language and advises me to proceed.

I ask the person facing the front of the room this question. She usually says "yes" and turns around. Now they are both facing the audience together. This doesn't mean that they have agreed on anything. It just means that they are standing shoulder-to-shoulder and are both facing the same direction and looking at the same thing. The great thing about this is that no one lost anything in this interchange. The person making the other one right lost nothing and the person who turned around lost nothing. It's very simple and no shields were put up. Communication has the possibility of continuing from this point because they are facing the same direction, they are standing together shoulder-to-shoulder and have, thereby, created the realm of possibility for communication to take place.

How do you make someone right? Here is a specific situation that you may have experienced as a manager.

Your boss has just told you that morale in your department is dropping and that you have to do something about it.

There are probably a million reasons why the morale is low and all of them, perhaps, outside your ability of changing. However, you do need to say something to the boss. You could connect with him or her on the emotional level by saying something to the effect:

"Yea, well whose fault is that?" Pretty brave statement but these are desperate times and people say desperate things. You might say, "I can't help it. My department thinks that they are the next group to be laid off." Or you might simply respond: "That's terrible."

The problem with responding at the emotional level, as illustrated above, is that you are connecting with your boss's

ego and when you do that, there's trouble ahead. Watch out! It's also a display of defeat on your part. Defeat is an attitude only, but when you've connected with someone's ego and they smell blood, well, you know what happens. It gets very messy and there are no winners.

If you catch yourself connecting at the emotional level, stop and re-start. It's really not that difficult to do. If you have just uttered one of the responses from above, catch yourself, and then say, "Wait a minute, that's not what I meant. Let me start over again." Then connect at the spiritual level. Here's how: Take step #1. Make the boss right--even if s/he is wrong by saying,

Step #1: "You're right, morale is low in my department."

You've just made the boss right and it was so simple. You've connected with him or her at the spiritual level. You have begun building a relationship--even if you never had one before. You have just laid a brick or another brick in the foundation of your relationship with the boss.

As a society we don't make people right very often. In fact we make them wrong more often than we make them right so if you make your boss right, they will probably be a little surprised--if not really surprised! It will feel right to your boss because you've touched the heart rather than the ego and people are much more into win-win situations when their heart has been touched rather than their ego. When

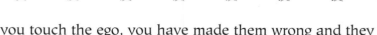

you touch the ego, you have made them wrong and they usually go into an attack or retreat mode.

Anytime you react at the emotional level and hear yourself saying, "that's too bad" or "that's just the way it is" or "we have to do it this way," you have just sapped your personal power because you have assumed a defeatist or victim role. You have just cut off the pipeline to access your personal power. You have put yourself in a lose-lose situation whether it be with the boss as in this situation, or with a co-worker or even a client in another situation. When we make people wrong, we may think we are more powerful, but that really isn't the case. You can't have power over anyone. When you make them right, there's a connection at a higher level where both of you can see the oneness between you and the possibility of creating something bigger and better.

Keep in mind that you want to respond in a charge neutral way. I will be using this term numerous times throughout the book, so let's take a look at what charge neutral means. It means that there is no charge to your voice what-so-ever. You are not charged up or down. There is a neutral tone to your voice. There is no excitement or sadness or any other type of expression to your voice. It is charge neutral. Kind of like the telephone computer voice when you call information for a number. You can say a lot more and you can get a lot more done when you use a charge neutral voice. People are more receptive and open to hearing things when the information comes in a charge neutral voice.

KEY INSIGHT: Keep in mind that there are people out there who have a need to be right and these folks never let their need to be right interfere with anyone else's truth or opinion. They can't see or hear where the other person is coming from. Even if someone else has a great idea or suggestion, the person who needs to be right won't hear it because he or she is caught up in protecting their "rightness." I can tell you from experience that trying to argue with someone like that is like trying to read the New York Times in a high wind. It's like we say in Texas, that dog ain't gonna hunt! Make people right, even if they are wrong. You can always put in the correction later and I will tell you how to do that.

When you make people right, even when they're wrong, both parties will feel good about that exchange. It creates the realm of possibility, the space for both of you to stand shoulder-to-shoulder and begin moving in the direction that you want to go.

Only you can determine how you respond or react to your business, your co-workers, your boss. You may be convinced that the other person is the cause of the problem or the problem is "out there" somewhere, or that the other person needs to change. It has nothing to do with them. It's all about you.

Here's a hypothetical situation which may not be so hypothetical. You've asked your administrative assistant to prepare some documents that you need quickly. She completes them and brings them into you. You begin to read and you catch some "typos" and some grammatical errors.

You ask her why she didn't run spell check and grammar check, and she says that she did. There's make wrong #1. Then you proceed to tell her that you need these documents right away and can't she understand that? That's make wrong #2. Then you proceed to tell her exactly how you want the changes made and when you want them and ask her to please do them right this time. That's make wrong #3. She goes off to make the corrections and in a short while returns with the documents. There are still some mistakes, and you go ballistic. Sound familiar? It's a story that is more familiar than many of us think. You begin to get really upset. Some strong words come out, and you are practically yelling. Your administrative assistant runs out of the room crying. How many "make wrongs" have you counted now? Plenty!

After the first make wrong that I identified above, the assistant didn't hear a single word you were telling her and she brought back the document to prove it. When you make people wrong, you diminish, and in this case, "blow" the relationship. She puts her shields up and nothing gets in. Productivity is greatly reduced. How long will it take for the assistant to come out of the bathroom, and for the two of you to be on talking terms--if she doesn't decide to quit?

Making people wrong is a destructive behavior. Making people right is a strong tool for building long-term relationships. Making people wrong comes from your head or your ego. Making people right comes from your heart. Stay in touch with your power source and create the realm of possibility for getting what you want by making people right.

When you make them wrong, they won't hear anything you have to say after that because they have their defenses up (shields). When you make them right, they can hear what you have to say next.

Think about this:

Making people right:
> creates the realm of possibility for you to have a relationship with the other person. When you make people right, you validate who they are at that particular moment. They feel heard and are more willing to hear what you have to say.

Part 1
Chapter 4
Ask Permission

"Just do it!"
NIKE

This is what I call being sensitive to where the person is or isn't in terms of being available to you. Asking permission is about becoming sensitive to how well a person is positioned to hear what you have to say next. Once you know they are listening to you, you then condition the conversation. It's a request to have a conversation. It's about asking permission rather than dumping on someone--and most of us are used to dumping on other people.

Dumping is when we communicate irresponsibly by just letting everything gush out such as (1) emotional reactions, (2) strong opinions that we have to have the other person get, (3) more information than what was asked for or needed.

Why do we do this? Well, it's that good old training that we have had for so long. We learned it as children and then it is carried into the workplace. Think back to when you were a "gopher" and your manager dumped on you. You swore you'd get even, and that you'd never do it to your employees. Well, now that you are a manager, are you dumping?

Few people ask permission to have a conversation and when we don't ask, communication stops. People may still be talking but effective communication has ceased. When you don't ask permission, your main focus is making a point, going for a result, and, perhaps, losing the relationship in the meantime.

You forget that results come from relationships and not the other way around. Results will come naturally and in their own time, provided that you developed the relationship first. Even if you tell me that you are right about a point you are trying to get across to someone, I will tell you that you may be right but you are not sensitive. You've put the result ahead of the relationship. You may be excellent in your job, but you may lose your staff because you are not sensitive to them. You may be excellent at your job but if you don't have a relationship with your boss, you may lose your job.

You must condition the conversation. Ask permission to have the conversation because when you do, you honor the other person's emotional boundaries. They may not know what you are doing, if they are not familiar with boundaries, but they will like it and feel good about it.

You have probably heard some of the "knock, knock" jokes going around. So if I say, "Knock, knock," you say, "Who's there?" You don't say, "Come in on!" No, you ask who is there first. You have set a boundary by asking who is there. The challenge for most of us these days is that we honor physical boundaries such as a closed door but we don't honor emotional boundaries. As I mentioned above, we just start talking or dumping whether the other person is ready or not. Such behavior does not lead to effective communication. It usually leads to resentment and an emotional reaction.

When you make people right, you honor who the person is and help them create a space in which the two of you can move the communication process forward. When you ask for permission, you are asking them if they are ready, willing and able to move forward with you in this particular conversation or to hear what you have to say next.

It's as if you have knocked on someone's door when you make them right and they then open the door but keep the chain lock on the door. At this point, you are only talking to them through the six inch opening in the door allowed by the chain lock. Not a very effective way to communicate but that's about as much space as we usually give ourselves in most business communications.

By asking permission, you are asking them to remove the chain lock and open the door completely. To do this, you must get a YES or a NO. If they say YES, proceed with the conversation. If they say NO, reschedule the conversation for another time. You want the other person to listen to what you have to say and be ready to hear it all. This doesn't necessarily mean that they are going to do what you ask them to do or even agree with you. The key is that they are listening fully and completely. They are positioned to hear what you have to say. Until they remove the chain lock by saying YES, they won't hear it all, if they are even willing to hear some of it.

So how does this work in a business situation. Here's the situation with the boss:

Your boss has just told you that morale in your department is dropping and that you have to do something about it.

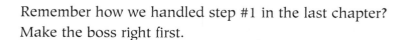

Remember how we handled step #1 in the last chapter?
Make the boss right first.

Step #1: "You're right. Morale is low in my department."

Now, here's how you ask permission:

Step #2: "May I tell you something?"

(Again, keep it charge neutral. No charge to your voice. Be
the telephone computer.)

Easy isn't is? Yes, it is easy, it's just not simple. Why?
Because we have been trained to violate people's emotional
boundaries by telling them what we think, what they should
do or just dumping on them without their permission. We
have so much information, data, knowledge that we feel it's
our job to tell people everything we know, even if they don't
ask, even if they don't want it. The armed forces are great at
violating this step, however, they are training people to
survive in combat situations and I would suppose life is
more important than relationships in a combat situation.
However, in business situations, if it is not a life or death
situation, use this step.

It really is the easiest step of the three. A simple question
and yet we forget or simply omit this step time and time
again and it is the most important step. Always ask for more
than enough permission.

KEY INSIGHT: You can really say a lot more and influence many more people, if you ask permission first. This step saves time, it saves you energy and it saves you upset.

Step #2, or asking for permission to have the conversation, is still not the place to give your ideas, advice or opinions. Here you are simply asking for permission to share your ideas or opinions during the conversation. You are not asking the other person to start or stop anything. You are simply asking permission to share your ideas or ask them something. It's short and sweet. Keep it that way! Don't confuse this step with asking them to do something. That is an entirely different issue and it is not done at this step.

As a business coach, people write me a check every single month so that I will coach them. Yet, I will always ask for more than enough permission before I tell my clients what I think or give my advice. It's interesting that when I do ask for permission to tell them something or make a request, my client might say, "Well, why do you think I'm paying you?" And I'll respond by making them right. "You're right, you do pay me for my advice. May I tell you what that is?" At this point, they usually just say, "yes."

You do not want to assume that they want to hear your comments or that they are ready to hear your comments. They must tell you that they are ready, willing and able to hear what you have to say by saying YES. They also have the choice of saying NO. That's fine, too. If they say NO, they are letting you know that now is not a good time.

You can set up a time later but you'll be wasting your time if you attempt to communicate now. By saying YES, they've taken the chain lock off the door and they are open to what you have to say.

KEY INSIGHT: Get a YES or a NO. Don't assume or think they are ready to hear you. Until they say YES, they won't hear what you have to say. Productivity decreases when you are trying to tell someone something and they are not able to hear it. Asking permission makes you more productive.

Think about this:

Asking permission:

> conditions the conversation. It allows the other person to create the space in order for them to hear all of what you have to say and all of what you are asking for. If you haven't conditioned the conversation by asking for permission, they may not hear it all and neither of you will get what you want.

Part 1
Chapter 5
Tell The Truth

"What lies behind us, and what lies before us are tiny matters, compared to what lies within us."

Ralph Waldo Emerson

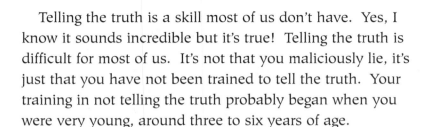

Telling the truth is a skill most of us don't have. Yes, I know it sounds incredible but it's true! Telling the truth is difficult for most of us. It's not that you maliciously lie, it's just that you have not been trained to tell the truth. Your training in not telling the truth probably began when you were very young, around three to six years of age.

Let me share a situation that happened to me that illustrates this point. Probably eight or ten years ago, I was talking to a group of women who had some small children with them. I was still relatively new to public speaking and, of course, I was nervous. When I get nervous, my hands sweat. Yes, that's right, they sweat--not perspire. In fact, they just drip water. So after my talk, some of the women came up to the front of the room to talk with me and while I was talking with them, I was trying to dry my hands on my skirt. One of the women had her little girl with her and as she was talking to me, the little girl took my hand in the most spontaneous and gentle way. Immediately she said, "Oh, your hand is wet." Well, of course, I could have just melted into the floor but before I had a chance to say or do anything, her mother said, "Don't say that. That's not nice."

Guess what? The little girl just had another lesson in NOT TELLING THE TRUTH and I suspect it wasn't her first and probably wasn't her last. We train our children not to tell the truth at a very young age. The sad part about this is that as we grow up and move into the work force, marriage, children, we have been so well trained in this arena, and so we continue using this technique even though it no longer serves us or others.

When I tell this story, some people shake their heads and agree with me and others say that the situation with the little girl was an isolated incident. Well, so much for isolated incidents: on a flight back from Laredo to Houston, there were two siblings, a boy and girl whom I would guess to be around 4 and 5 years old. The children wanted to see the propeller so the mother and father sat in the two seats in front of them. The little boy, Bryan, was precious. The flight attendant came by and told "Kitty," the little girl, that she had to keep her seat belt fastened at all times. The little boy responded to the flight attendant with, "She doesn't know any better." And that was the truth for Bryan. The flight attendant said, "Well, she better know better." Not only did the flight attendant make Bryan wrong, she also gave him the message that it was not OK to tell his truth. My, oh, my! Training begins early.

As a manager, you may have heard about a situation similar to the one I will illustrate or perhaps this actually happened to you. I know this has happened to me when I worked in the corporate job.

The situation:

One of your employees who has worked for you for more than three years is basically a poor employee. He just doesn't do the work well. Today is the day that you could no longer tolerate his work. He really messed up and you want to fire him right on the spot. You go to your boss and tell her of the situation. She questions you about this employee's past performance and you kind of "hem and haw" so she asks why you haven't said anything before now. She pulls out the performance reviews and as she looks at them, there's a puzzled look on her face. She asks you why you have given this employee overall reviews for the last three years that say he's doing fine? You begin to feel a little red in the face and finally have to tell her the truth: "I didn't want to get anyone mad."

The bottom line here is that if you are not telling the truth, are you really communicating effectively? Little white lies have a tendency to turn into huge messes that you will have to deal with sooner or later.

As in the above situation, whatever is "your" truth, you have learned to hide it or do something else. You are only willing to say what you believe will be acceptable and you "stuff" the rest of it. As time goes on, no one really sees the real you. No one knows who you really are because you have not said your truth. It may have been someone else's truth but it wasn't yours. So you lose yourself. You recognize yourself by who you are, what you say and what you do. Other people recognize you the same way. If you have not been telling your truth, who are you? Do you really know yourself and do others really know you?

If you don't know who you are, you may put up a barrier between you and others in order to protect yourself from who other people think you are. Once that barrier goes up, it is tough to take it down. But down it will come when you begin to tell the truth as you know it. When you tell the

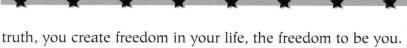

truth, you create freedom in your life, the freedom to be you. Telling the truth will set you free to be in relationship with people, opening the door to letting people see and hear who you really are.

Telling the truth is what builds lasting relationships between yourself and another. Telling the truth creates trust and trust creates safety and confidence. When someone feels safe and has confidence in you, they are much more willing to create bigger and more results faster and easier. If you are not telling the truth, the relationship becomes a struggle. Be willing to tell the truth as you know it. It's not what you think the internal or external client wants to hear-- it's the truth as you know it.

Wouldn't it have been better for the mother to have allowed me to be responsible for dealing with my issues around nerves and sweaty hands, rather than making her little girl responsible? Telling the truth allows everyone to be responsible for themselves. When we say what we think someone wants to hear, we are being responsible for their feelings and how they act. That's not our job--especially in the work place.

We've been trained to do other things rather than tell the truth. They may be similar to the truth but they're not the truth and they don't contribute to long-term relationships, to increased productivity or profitability. Why do you think CEOs hire executive coaches? Because they need someone who will tell them the truth. Their executive committee has been trained not to tell the truth.

Here are some things we do rather than tell the truth:

The Truth vs. Accuracy

We tend to be accurate rather than telling the truth. Truth is a skill. Accuracy is a measure. The truth can change and still be true. Accuracy is accuracy. Something can be true and inaccurate and something can be accurate and not be true. The truth is better. Accuracy contributes to telling the truth. Tell the truth.

The Truth vs. Comparison

We tend to compare ourselves or others rather than tell the truth. The truth stands on its own without having to relate to the past or the future. When you compare, it means that you need to refer to how you used to be or what you are going to do or be, so it's dependent on some other measure. Tell the truth as it is today, at this very moment. If you compare, it's disempowering. When I have talked about this concept before, someone in the group has said, "Linda, I came out on the high side of the comparison!" I tell them that I'm happy for them, ask them if I can tell them what I think and then, after receiving permission, say that it's really a false sense of accomplishment. Tell the truth.

The Truth vs. Evidence

We tend to gather evidence rather than telling the truth. Evidence is what you create that may not be true. You can prove your point and show evidence of why someone else is wrong, make yourself right and that's ego driven. The truth is just the way it is at that particular moment. It is empowering. Tell the truth.

The Truth vs. Withholding

We withhold information rather than telling the truth. When you tell your truth in the moment in a sticky situation, you may think that this will hurt someone's feelings, or perhaps it will sound unkind. By keeping your voice charge neutral, you are sharing your truth rather than making someone wrong. If you don't tell your truth, you are withholding important information from them. You don't help anyone by withholding something. By withholding, you put the relationship in jeopardy. You have an energy drain because it takes lots of energy to keep secrets or keep all the information in your emotional file rather than theirs.

Withholding can be a power play. When you withhold, and you are successful at it, you may be able to get people to do what you want them to do. However, it is a game and not a healthy game and sooner or later, they will find out and the relationship will be damaged. When you say it all and do not withhold, you will have more free time because you won't be worrying about what you didn't say. You truly value and honor yourself and the other person when you say it all by telling the truth and withholding nothing. Tell the truth.

Be willing to recognize and accept what is true in order to see things as they are in the present moment. When you live in the present moment, it is easier to tell the truth because you are not dealing with fear: fear about living in the past or the future. Living in the present moment takes courage and so does telling the truth.

44

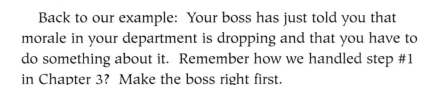
Back to our example: Your boss has just told you that morale in your department is dropping and that you have to do something about it. Remember how we handled step #1 in Chapter 3? Make the boss right first.

Step #1: "You're right. Morale is low in my department."

Then you asked permission to proceed with the conversation by saying,

Step #2: "May I tell you something?"

Now comes step #3 where you tell the truth. You tell the truth regardless of the circumstances--mindful of the consequences and you tell the truth as you know it to be right now.

Step #3: "Morale may go lower and turn-over increase unless we can help these people see that there is a place for them in this organization and I'm not sure how to do that."

★ ★ ★ ★ ★ ★ ★ ★

My words are not necessarily the only way to say it. These are my responses and it may be what you say or not. These are my words and my truth. They may not be your words or your truth. Your truth may be different than mine. You may know how to help employee morale. If so, tell your truth. Here is an opportunity to write your own response:

Step #1: _____

Step #2: _____

Step #3: _____

You may have to repeat the process several times during the conversation because the other person may be seducing you into reverting back to communicating at the emotional level and that is a huge energy drain. Stay at the spiritual level by repeating the process, as many times as necessary.

In our example: You respond to the boss's comment about morale being low in your department.

Step #1: "You're right. Morale is low in my department."

Step #2: "May I tell you something?"

Step #3: "Morale may go lower and turn-over increase unless we can help these people see that there is a place for them in this organization and I'm not sure how to do that."

Now, if the boss responds to this by saying, "Well, you better figure it out soon or you may be out of a job," that's a threat and it is communicating at the emotional level. Stay at the spiritual level by responding,

Step #1: "You are right. I may be out of a job."

Step #2: "May I ask you something?"

Step #3: "Am I in this alone or will you help me?"

Your boss may say, "It's all up to you. I don't know how to tell you to begin."

You respond by saying,

Step #1: "Thanks for being honest with me."

Step #2: "May I tell you something?"

Step #3: "I think I'll call in an expert."

It's the truth and it's simple. Now, this is just one truth-- my truth. Your truth in this situation may be different so I've left room for you to add in your language. Don't gather evidence about how it's not as bad as it was or compare your department with another department. Tell the truth as you know it.

Your language:

Step #1: _____

Step #2: _____

Step #3: _____

   And finally, remember Bryan from the airplane flight? Just to remind us that children always tell the truth and we can learn from them, here's the final story. As I mentioned, Bryan was sitting directly in back of his Dad. At one point, Bryan said, "Dad, I see the hole in your head." Well, as I was seated behind and to the left of Bryan and his Dad, I could only see the side of "Dad's" head. However, when Dad turned back around completely to face forward--guess what? Dad did have a "hole in his head." You and I might call it a bald spot. The truth for Bryan was "a hole in the head." Children tell us the truth. Too bad we don't let them keep the skill of telling the truth.

Think about this:

When you tell the truth:
> you are communicating effectively. You are having a true conversation rather than trying to seduce or manipulate someone into doing something for you. Telling the truth is about creating freedom in your life and, especially, in your work.

48

Part 1
Chapter 6
Reasons that block the use of Business Finesse

"The only thing we have to fear is fear itself."
Franklin D. Roosevelt

Reason #1: FEAR

Mark Twain said that his life had been filled with terrible calamities, most of which never happened. I can see the truth in what Mr. Twain says, however, when we are in the middle of the infamous alligator swamp, we forget about Mr. Twain and focus on getting out of there with our life. In fact, at that point, fear takes over and we lose all sense of direction, all sense of purpose so we usually get eaten by the alligators, or did someone say "sharks?" Generally, fear happens when we don't have our needs taken care of on a regular basis. Don't get me wrong, fear, as in a gun to your head, is a real threat to your safety and that fear is a normal and appropriate response. However, the fear that I'm talking about here is the ego-based fear that stops us from achieving what we really want. In fact, it usually stops us before we even get started. This fear began in the past and you have carried it around with you all these years. It's time to recognize it and give it up.

Physiological Reactions to Fear

When we experience fear, several physiological things happen such as sweaty palms (that's _my_ favorite), increased heart rate (for no apparent reason), shaky knees and hands and even your voice, inability to speak or speak coherently, decreased ability to take actions (remember the swamp). These are the physiological reactions to fear and they are reactions not responses. When you react to fear, you create stress and conflict. It's an emotional energy drain. I will tell you more about how to respond to fear later.

A reaction to fear comes from the ego. It's not real, but we perceive it to be, so we have a reaction. The reactions don't really make us feel better, but that's all the ego knows how to do. There is a better way, as I mentioned, and I'll get to that after I tell you about the origins of fear.

Origins of Fear

There are several origins of fear. The one that impacts most of us is the *first time syndrome*. This is the fear that most of us experience anytime we do something for the first time. After we've done it once or perhaps several times, it gets easier and fear disappears. I think back to the first time I gave a public presentation. I experienced so much fear that I could hardly speak. I had to read from my notes. The second time I gave a public talk, my hands were sweating, but I could speak that time. The third time was even easier and now, after hundreds of public presentations-- "it's a piece of cake!"

Another origin is the *lie*. A lie is always an origin of fear. What if you get caught? What will people think? What will people do? The lie usually occurs when who you are now is not equal to who you want to be, and so you lie. This is a very subtle origin of fear but an excellent origin if you take the time to really think about it.

The reason we don't tell the truth or say it all is about consequences, whether they are positive or negative. A *perceived consequence* is another origin of fear. This happens when you think about the worst thing happening to you and

your mind, or ego, can't recover from that thought. If the worst case scenario happens, you may die--or so your ego believes. So the ego steps in at this point and shuts your systems down. If you feel slowed down or stopped in an endeavor, and you are not certain why, it could be fear and the origin could be a perceived consequence. The interesting part of this is that most perceived consequences are not real but the ego makes them appear real. So we are stopped dead in our tracks. We don't take the risks to build the business we want, to communicate at the level we want, to put our integrity first. It's a very vicious cycle, and it can be stopped.

One origin of fear that has haunted people for years is being *ahead of yourself.* Your goals or material dreams are too big or too drastic for you to hold onto for very long. Your "havingness" level is not high enough. Think of the people who win the big LOTTO jackpot and then are penniless before the year is out. They can't hold onto the money. The bottom line is that they really don't know what to do with the things that they received (money) even though they wanted them. The quick solution is to be careful for what you ask. You might get it sooner than you really wanted and this thought creates fear.

The last origin that I want to talk about is *immobility.* Unfortunately, there are people out there who are stuck in a rut and the energy it takes for them to get moving out of that rut is simply too great. So it's better for them to stay in the rut rather than move out of it. Think back to starting your exercise routine on Monday. You went to the club to work out and you were really sore on Tuesday. So Wednesday morning rolls around, and you are wondering if you should get up to work out. Your body is sore. Maybe you should just take the day off. This is immobility. However, if you got up and went to the club to work out, you might get enough energy going to move into momentum where you are exercising on a regular basis without even thinking about it. Immobility is what stops most people from learning and using a new skill. It's easier to stay with the old way of communicating or the old way of being.

Ways to Eliminate Fear
• As NIKE says, "just do it!" When you just do it, it moves you past immobility and gets the momentum flowing.

• Feel the fear and include it as you move forward. Yes, it's scary but it's a great way to learn to trust yourself and take risks. Life is about taking risks and until we all become highly evolved spiritual beings, fear will probably always be lurking around somewhere. So get used to it. As they say, "dance with your demons."

• Remove the ego from the scene by not making the thing that you fear personal. In other words, look at it as simply practice. I tell people to go out and practice being a great communicator. If you make a mistake, no big deal. It was just practice, anyway, so try it again and practice it again!

The same is true with relationships. Practice with a relationship. People think that as soon as they meet someone and there's chemistry, this is the ultimate relationship. Unfortunately, they find out differently three months later. Instead of committing to a relationship, perhaps they might have committed to practice. Doing it this way means that you don't have to take the relationship personally--yet!

At some point in our earlier years, the ego got involved with our lives in order to keep us alive. We no longer need the ego to do that for us but it's still around trying. Think back to when you were first learning how to ride a two wheeler bike instead of the four wheeler. If you were like me, you got on that bike, your Dad pushed you and you fell over. You got back on that bike, your Dad pushed you and you fell over. After doing that at least three dozen times, perhaps you rode! If I had taken falling off that bike personally, I never would have ridden and neither would you. You don't need to take anything personally. Depersonalize the situation and eliminate the ego.

• Break the whole project down into baby steps and start here. Many of us tackle huge projects and we usually become overwhelmed. Fear shows up and we are stopped dead in our tracks. We don't complete anything, much less get started.

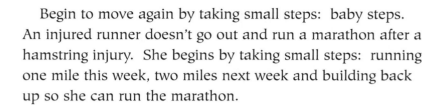

Begin to move again by taking small steps: baby steps. An injured runner doesn't go out and run a marathon after a hamstring injury. She begins by taking small steps: running one mile this week, two miles next week and building back up so she can run the marathon.

By breaking the project down into small steps, you can handle it. For example, if you need to terminate an employee, many times we may create so much fear that we really blow the whole thing out of proportion, say things we don't really mean to the employee and perhaps go beyond the legal limits, unknowingly. What if you broke down the process on a sheet of paper and said something like "today I will do this" and "tomorrow I will do that." "Next week I will handle this," etc. By breaking it down to baby steps, it's manageable and you eliminate the ego.

Dr. Henry C. Link said, "I venture to say that at the bottom of most fear, both mild and severe, will be found an overactive mind and an underactive body. Hence, I have advised many people, in their quest for happiness, to use their heads less and their arms and legs more--in useful work and play."

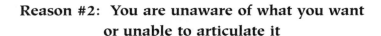

Reason #2: You are unaware of what you want or unable to articulate it

When I have coached individuals or have given presentations to audiences, many times I ask them what they want and most of the time, people can only tell me one or two things that they want. One person actually told me eight things that she wanted but was stopped at eight. Isn't it amazing that we can only think of and articulate two to eight things that we want?

Stop for a second and articulate out loud what you want. How many did you come up with? Interesting, isn't it?

Physiological Reasons for the Inability to Articulate What You Want

You've felt it before: the upset stomach, the headache. Perhaps you even snapped at the kids or spouse this morning. Your spouse asks you what is wrong and you say, "I don't know!?" It happens when you are not able to articulate what you want. Why? My personal belief is that you have stuffed so many feelings, ideas, creations, as a child, and, today, the result of stuffing is a feeling of the upset tummy, headache, etc. Today as an adult, you automatically stuff things without even knowing it and you simply feel the physiological reactions. Now, I'm not a doctor and don't ever want to be, but in listening to my own body's intelligence, this is what is true for me. I suspect it is probably true for a lot of other people. You may want something or have an idea that you want to articulate, but

★ ★ ★ ★ ★ ★ ★ ★

you are so well trained to stuff it that all you feel is the reaction. Connect the reaction to what's really going on, and you might be surprised.

Origins for the Inability to Articulate What You Want

The plain and honest truth is that you don't *know what you want,* and if you don't know what you want, you'll never be able to articulate it. You were trained as a child not to want or need, and you learned quite well. As you sat in the shopping cart going down the grocery isles with your mother, you kept telling her what you wanted and she kept saying NO. You became trained NOT to ask for what you wanted, especially in the grocery store. I've coached thousands of individuals who don't know what they want, and these are business chiefs, business owners, artists, authors, highly intelligent and highly educated people, and they don't know what they want.

Ways to Eliminate the Inability to Articulate What You Want

• Start wanting a lot! That's easy to say but a little difficult to do. So here's how to do it. Get in touch with everything that makes you smile. You can do that by playing a game called, **The 75 Things That Make Me Smile**. Use the format shown on page 59. This form is also found in the Appendix if you want to make additional copies. Or take a regular sized sheet of paper and divide it into 3 columns. The heading for the first column is "Things That Make Me Smile When I Do Them By Myself." Then number 1 through 25 underneath. The heading for the second column is "Things That Make Me Smile When I Do Them With One

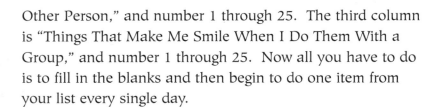
Other Person," and number 1 through 25. The third column is "Things That Make Me Smile When I Do Them With a Group," and number 1 through 25. Now all you have to do is to fill in the blanks and then begin to do one item from your list every single day.

Get to know everything that makes you smile. It's usually things that you already have. Your car, your job, your business, your friends, projects, hobbies. As you get in touch with these, you get more in tune with what you really want and then are able to articulate that. If you do something from your list and it doesn't make you smile, erase it and put something else in its place that will make you smile.

I promise that you will begin to say to yourself, "Yes, that's what I want!" and then you'll begin to say it out loud. That's the turning point to get you on your way to articulating what it is you want.

★   ★   ★   ★   ★   ★   ★   ★

Things that Make Me Smile When I Do Them By Myself	Things That Make Me Smile When I Do Them With One Other Person	Things That Make Me Smile When I Do Them With A Group
1	1.	1.
2.	2.	2.
3.	3.	3.
4	4.	4.
5.	5.	5.
6.	6.	6.
7.	7.	7.
8.	8.	8.
9.	9.	9.
10.	10.	10.
11.	11.	11.
12.	12.	12.
13.	13.	13.
14.	14.	14.
15.	15.	15.
16.	16.	16.
17.	17.	17.
18.	18.	18.
19.	19.	19.
20.	20.	20.
21.	21.	21.
22.	22.	22.
23.	23.	23.
24.	24.	24.
25.	25.	25.

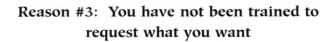

Reason #3: You have not been trained to request what you want

Even if you know what you want, are you willing to request it?

Physiological Reactions of Not Being Able to Make Requests
You have an emptiness in the pit of your stomach, you are tired a lot, you don't look people in the eye and you speak in hushed tones. In other words, you are very reserved, laid back to the point that people notice it as a weakness. It might even show up on your performance review. Not being able to request what you want probably has a lot of anger attached to it but you won't see it, it's buried too deep--but it might manifest as an ulcer, chronic fatigue, extreme sadness. Many people today call it depression. It's probably extreme sadness.

Origins of Not Being Able to Request What You Want
You probably were a sensitive child and a lot of things, mostly words, hurt you. You were trained not to *question authority figures*. You probably came from a home that did not honor individual differences. It was safer to keep your head low and your opinions to yourself. Basically, you were taught that "this is the way we've always done it and nothing is going to change and if you question the authority figure, you might get hit or yelled at." It wasn't safe to be you or ask for what you needed. So you did the best you could without asking. You grew up by cause and effect and that's how you learned. You may still be using the same method to learn today but it's not effective.

Ways to Eliminate the Inability to Make Requests

• Begin to make a lot of requests!

A request is something you say or do which is FOR something. A request usually means the person (employee, boss, customer) will take an action or stop an action in order to get or have something that wasn't there before. Requests to stop or start are both valid and useful.

The trick to making requests is that you must be willing to make requests. You must know what to request and you must have the language to request. You might say, "Would you be willing to stop interrupting me?" Or "Would you be willing to complete the report and have it on my desk by 3 pm Wednesday?"

• Begin requesting in "low-risk" areas. Low-risk areas are areas that you feel safe. These areas may or may not be with your family. They may be with friends or your spouse. The key is that you feel safe with that person and you feel safe when you begin practicing requesting what you want. By requesting first in low-risk areas, you get to practice making the request, sometimes getting and sometimes not getting what you requested. It is a way to build self-confidence and self-esteem.

Requesting what you want is about being fully responsible and detaching from other people's thoughts, wishes, desires and focusing on exactly what you want.

Make requests whenever you need something, when you want something, when someone isn't producing or when it's time for a change in how things operate. You may not get it all, but you will get a lot more than someone who didn't make the request.

Reason #4: You are unable to say it all or tell the truth

Physiological Reactions of Not Being Able to Say It All or Tell the Truth

You have cotton-mouth and you feel jittery. You begin to perspire on your forehead and your body starts to ache. You have a strong desire to run away somewhere, anywhere, where no one can find you.

Origins of Not Being Able to Say It All or Tell the Truth

You have been trained to tell people *what they want to hear* or what you believe they want to hear. This training begins quite early, when you were four to five years old. See Chapter 5.

Ways to Eliminate Not Being Able to Say It All or Tell the Truth

• Tell the truth as you know it regardless of what anybody else thinks or says. This is not an opportunity to be vindictive or cruel. This is simply your opportunity to say it all and tell your truth. It must be what you sincerely, in your heart, believe to be true rather than gossip from what you

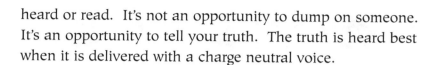

heard or read. It's not an opportunity to dump on someone.
It's an opportunity to tell your truth. The truth is heard best
when it is delivered with a charge neutral voice.

• Be willing to take a stand for your truth. If you do this
with a charge neutral voice, people are more likely to hear
what your stand is and why you are standing for your truth.
A stand comes from the word "standard" and it means what
you will now stand for. You can stand for your truth or
someone else's truth but it is a stand. Don't stand for what
you think someone else's ideas, truths or opinions are. Know
what you stand for and when you know this, you will be able
to tell the truth about it and say it all.

Think about this:

There are several things that can block you
from achieving Business Finesse, the most
common one being fear. We all have it. We
simply need to be aware of it and deal with it.

Part 1
Chapter 7
The Formula for Business Finesse

"In every work of genius we recognize our own rejected thoughts."

Goethe

Some people enjoy the concept of formulas. It's something they can see and work with rather than an idea. So here is the formula for Business Finesse. The formula gives you the components necessary for you to achieve the result, Business Finesse. Let me give you an example before I talk about Business Finesse. Take the formula for momentum. In order to create momentum, you need to have an idea, a purpose and action. When you have these three things, you create momentum.

Momentum = Idea + Purpose + Action

If you are missing one of the components, it's much more difficult to reach momentum, if you ever do. So it's just like we learned in algebra class. You've got to use the entire equation. When you use the entire equation, you create the result you want. Here's the formula for Business Finesse:

Business Finesse = awareness + language + practice

Awareness.   There are several things you need to be aware of. You need to be aware of what's blocking you from using Business Finesse. What belief systems do you have that are no longer true or no longer serve you? See Chapter 6 for more information on the reasons that block Business Finesse. You need to be aware of what level you are "communicating at" with someone--the emotional or spiritual level. See Chapter 2. You also need to be aware of the three step process for achieving Business Finesse. See Chapter 2.

Language.   Language is an important part of the formula because if you don't have the right words at the right time, you won't feel good about the communication and you probably won't get what you want. Most people are stopped or blocked because they don't have the language they need to get what they want.

Many people hire me as their coach in order to give them language that they can use until they can begin to develop language on their own. That is part of the reason I wrote, **Business Finesse: How to Say the Right Thing at the Right Time**. My clients needed language and as I gave it to them during our coaching calls, they asked me if I could FAX the language to them. Well, I couldn't then but what I did do was write the book and they bought it. They bought it because they needed language and that's what I gave them. I don't care if it's the baby-sitter or the CEO, we all need language. Managers especially need language.

When you are telling the truth, making a request, you need language. Think of the time you wanted Suzy Q or Joe Smith to tell somebody something. They never did tell "somebody" something and you were mad because they didn't. Did you ever think about why they didn't tell "somebody" something? It was probably because they didn't have the language to do it. You just told them to do it but you didn't tell them what to say so they didn't say anything at all. The trick is to make certain they have the language they need, just as you need language to master the skill of Business Finesse. I'll be giving you lots of language in

Part II of this book. There are 50 situations that take you through the three step process and it gives you the language so you can achieve what you really want. There is even a space for you to add your own language.

Practice. I know, I know. It's a horrible word because most of us hate to practice. We just want to be a Michael Jordan, an Arnold Schwarzenegger or a Cindy Crawford instantly. Do you really think they got the bodies they have or the careers they have without practicing? Come on now, tell the truth. These folks practice a lot! In order to master Business Finesse, you will need to practice, also. Think back to the two wheel bike, it did take practice to ride it. You didn't get on it and ride the first time. Neither did I. However, as adults, we think we should read or see something once and then be able to do it perfectly. Not in the real world. Even good sex takes practice. Why should good business communication be any different? As Jim Rohn said, "With formal education you can earn a living, with self-education, you can earn a fortune." Practice is self-education. Start now!

Think about this:

Business Finesse = Awareness+Language+Practice

Part 2
Chapter 8
Sticky Situations in the Workplace

"The transformation of everyday work and life experience into language is the work of the soul and it takes practice."

Linda Talley

To master a skill requires time and practice. It also requires patience. It has been said that practice is compulsory education. Be willing to memorize these scripts and use them until you begin to have language flow naturally. I have left blank spaces at the end of each situation. If your language is different, add your own language and use that to practice. The key word here is to practice. The skill of riding a two wheeler bike, the skill of tying your shoe laces took a while for you to learn. Why should the skill of Business Finesse be any different?

Here are some situations taken from real-life management scenarios. The managers who shared some of these situations with me are listed in the "Thanks" section at the beginning of the book. Each situation is identified and explained along with the language that I would use for the three step process of Business Finesse. You then have the opportunity to write your own language.

We do ourselves a disservice when we discount our own thoughts, our feelings, our own language or bow down to experts or anyone else's point of view. You know the situation best. You know the boss, the employee, the client. Use your language if you feel more comfortable with it. The key is to use the three step process because that works.

You must not think that following expert advice or the language given automatically means that you have no self-trust. I call it granting power to a relationship. Grant power to our relationship by using the language that I give you or

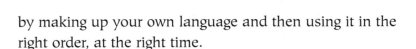
by making up your own language and then using it in the right order, at the right time.

Be willing to repeat this process several times during the conversation. If you don't you may be letting the other person seduce you into communicating at the emotional level. When that occurs, it's an emotional drain, a waste of time and it puts up walls between you, your employees and your clients. Keep practicing this process. It will get easier.

What usually happens when you keep the communication at the spiritual level is that the person may come back and say,
> "yes, but . . . . ." then say,
> "yes, and . . . ." then say,
> "yes, if . . . . ." and finally,
> "yes."

You will get to the same sort of YES as long as you use the three steps of Business Finesse.

There are three sections to Part II.
1. Sticky Situations: Dealing with your employees (internal clients).
2. Sticky Situations: Dealing with the boss (internal client).
3. Sticky Situations: Dealing with external clients (your customers).

SECTION 1: Dealing With Employees

1. Staying in Touch with Previous Staff/Associates

People leave your employ or the company all the time. They may leave for a good opportunity or get "forced" out. There are people that you may really want to stay in touch with--the up and comers, the innovators. Just because they didn't work out at your company doesn't mean that they don't have an awful lot of usefulness somewhere else. Stay in touch. It's OK. With FAX, e-mail and telephone, it's quite easy to stay connected. The problem is that you feel uncomfortable calling after this person has left the company. There is a way to reconnect. After you say hello, follow the steps.

Step #1: You are a pretty smart cookie to recognize a better opportunity for yourself.

Step #2: Can I tell you something?

Step #3: I'm really interested in staying in touch with you and hearing what you are up to. You are someone I'd like to keep in my rolodex as a resource.

OR

Step #1: You're an innovator.

Step #2: May I tell you something?

Step #3: I think you are going places and I want to stay in touch and be able to use you as a resource and vice versa.

Your language:

Step #1: _____

Step #2: _____

Step #3: _____

2. Dealing with a Disruptive Staff Member

Combative, argumentative, disruptive people are a challenge, especially when they are in your department. During your staff meetings, this particular person is interrupting other staff members--not necessarily you. Before the next staff meeting, you have a chat with this person. Keep this very charge neutral!

Step #1: You have a lot of interesting ideas that come to you during our staff meetings.

Step #2: May I share something with you?

Step #3: Do you realize that you are interrupting other people during our meetings?

The person says that he/she didn't realize that and you begin the process again.

Step #1: You're right, I didn't think you realized it. (If that is true.)

Step #2: May I ask you something?

Step #3: Would you be willing to hear people out completely before offering your ideas?

The person agrees and you begin the process again.

Step #1: Thank you for agreeing to do that.

Step #2: May I ask you one other thing?

Step #3: If you do interrupt someone in the future, may I stop you?

Your language:

Step #1: _____

Step #2: _____

Step #3: _____

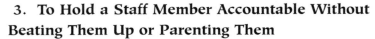

3. To Hold a Staff Member Accountable Without Beating Them Up or Parenting Them

If a staff member asks you to hold them accountable, it's a set-up. Don't accept the request. Here's what to do.

Step #1: You are someone who wants to achieve results.

Step #2: May I tell you something?

Step #3: I'm willing to set up a time to talk with you daily to hear the status report.

OR

Step #1: You are right to find a way to hold yourself accountable.

Step #2: May I ask you something?

Step #3: What five action steps are you going to take on a daily basis in order to get the project completed?

Your language:

Step #1: _____

Step #2: _____

Step #3: _____

4. Dealing with A Staff Member Who "Vents"

A certain staff member comes into your office at least once a week to vent about what is NOT going on "out there."

Step #1: You have the ability to see what needs to take place.

Step #2: May I ask you something?

Step #3: How can you be the model for getting more accomplished "out there?"

OR

Step #1: You have some strong opinions about what needs to change here.

Step #2: May I ask you something?

Step #3: What workable ideas can you come up with by Friday in order to reduce the stress around here and reduce the number of hours?

Your language:

Step #1: _____

Step #2: _____

Step #3: _____

5. An Employee Feels Unfairly Treated

One of your employees thinks he is being given the hardest work all the time and wants a break. As a manager, you believe that you are giving equal work to everyone. You say to him:

Step #1: You probably think you are doing the hardest work.

Step #2: May I tell you something?

Step #3: You are the one that I can count on to do it right the first time and then show others how to do it.

OR

Step #1: You are really feeling put upon, right?

Step #2: May I tell you something?

Step #3: Everyone here is carrying the same load.

Your language:

Step #1: _____

Step #2: _____

Step #3: _____

6. An Employee's Erratic Behavior

You notice a personality change in one of your employees and their productivity decreases. Your other employees are beginning to complain about this person. You suspect a drug problem but you have seen no evidence of it.

Step #1: Joe, you have been the best lineman I have ever worked with.

Step #2: Can I tell you something?

Step #3: Something about you has changed. I don't know what it is and I'm going to be watching you carefully. I won't let you hurt yourself on my shift.

OR

Step #1: Jane, you have been the backbone of this group ever since we began.

Step #2: May I tell you something?

Step #3: Something is going on with you and I don't know for sure what it is and I have my suspicions. Take care of this situation or I will have to take further action.

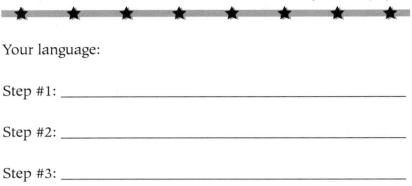

Your language:

Step #1: _____

Step #2: _____

Step #3: _____

7. Socializing After Hours With the Staff

A group of your employees is going out for beer after work. You have heard them planning it and know that they are going to ask you to attend, but you already have other plans. When they come to invite you, you say:

Step #1: What a great idea and way to have some fun this evening.

Step #2: May I tell you something?

Step #3: I already have plans, otherwise, I would be there with you.

OR

Step #1: You folks are smart to include the boss.

Step #2: May I tell you something?

Step #3: I have already made other plans for this evening and will have to miss this one.

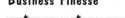

Your language:

Step #1: _____

Step #2: _____

Step #3: _____

8. An Employee Becomes Too Dependent on Your Help

One of your employees keeps asking you for help and you have helped him on several situations. You get the feeling that you are being a crutch for the employee rather than a manager.

Step #1: Stan, I hired you because you said you liked to work independently.

Step #2: May I ask you something?

Step #3: Why has that seemed to change now that you are working for me?

OR

Step #1: Jo Ellen, you have shown me how well you work on the independent projects that I have given you in the past.

Step #2: May I ask you something?

Step #3: Tell my why you seem to need more outside help now than before.

79

Your language:

Step #1: _____

Step #2: _____

Step #3: _____

9. Vacation Schedule for Employees

You have four people working in your department with you and you have just found out that three of them have scheduled vacation time during the last two weeks of the month leaving you by yourself. You call them into your office to discuss the situation.

Step #1: Each of you deserves a long vacation.

Step #2: May I share a situation that has come up?

Step #3: Each of you has scheduled your vacation time at exactly the same time leaving me here to run the shop. I can't do it by myself. How do you want to handle this?

OR

Step #1: Each of you has worked hard this year and you are due for a vacation.

Step #2: Can I tell you something?

Step #3: I need someone to help me during those two weeks. How do you suggest we handle this? What can be done?

Your language:

Step #1: _____

Step #2: _____

Step #3: _____

10. An Employee is Non-productive

One of your employees never completes a project on time. You have counseled with him on numerous occasions and nothing has worked. You are getting pressure from the rest of your department because the other staff members are tired of taking up the slack. Your next conversation with this employee goes something like:

Step #1: You have many positive qualities that make you an ideal member of this department. (Say this, if it's true.)

Step #2: Can I tell you something?

Step #3: One area that you must improve immediately is your ability to complete projects within the given time frame. I don't know how to tell you how to do this. It's up to you to figure this out and make changes in your routine.

If the employees says "I'll try." You respond at the spiritual level by saying:

Step #1: You're right. You really do want to try.

Step #2: May I tell you something?

Step #3: You will have to make the changes immediately if you want to stay in this department.

Your language:

Step #1: _____

Step #2: _____

Step #3: _____

11. The Employee Dress Code

Your boss has mentioned that Jane/Joe is not following the dress code. You have told her that you will follow up with Jane/Joe.

Step #1: Jane, you have an incredible sense of style and your outfits show it.

Step #2: May I share something with you?

Step #3: While lovely, they don't comply with our dress code of _____. Would you be willing to follow our code beginning tomorrow?

OR

Step #1: Joe, you look like someone out of Gentlemen's Quarterly.

Step #2: May I tell you something?

Step #3: Our dress code requires a suit and tie daily.

Your language:

Step #1: _____

Step #2: _____

Step #3: _____

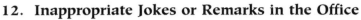

12. Inappropriate Jokes or Remarks in the Office

You have overheard one of your employees tell an off-colored joke or remark. Most in the group laughed but you didn't feel good about it. You say to the joke-teller (off-line):

Step #1: You have a way of making people laugh and feel good.

Step #2: May I share something with you?

Step #3: That joke wasn't your best and I only want your best.

If the employee says that everyone laughed, you can say:

Step #1: You are right. Everyone else laughed.

Step #2: May I tell you something?

Step #3: I didn't.

Your language:

Step #1: _____

Step #2: _____

Step #3: _____

13. Employee to Employee Conflicts

One of your employees comes into your office to complain to you about her office suite-mate. She tells you that this person is always making personal calls and interrupting her day so she is not as effective as she can be. Your comments to this employee:

Step #1: It's difficult to get things done when someone is distracting you.

Step #2: May I ask you something?

Step #3: Have you asked her to stop?

If she says no because she didn't think she should, you might say:

Step #1: You are right. It's not your job to tell her what to do.

Step #2: Do you want to know how I would handle this?

Step #3: Tell her that you know she's very busy and ask her if she would be willing to help you be more productive by making her personal calls after 5 pm.

Your language:

Step #1: _____

Step #2: _____

Step #3: _____

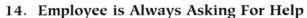

14. Employee is Always Asking For Help

One of your employees keeps bringing you problems without trying to figure them out first. You feel like a fireman/woman putting out fires. The next time he brings a problem to you, you say:

Step #1: You are someone who is quick to spot a problem.

Step #2: May I ask you something?

Step #3: Would you be willing to solve this problem on your own before you bring it to me?

If he says, "I have tried to solve it," you might say:

Step #1: Good for you!

Step #2: May I tell you something?

Step #3: Next time a problem arises, bring me three ways to solve the problem and we will solve it together based on your recommendations.

Your language:

Step #1: _____

Step #2: _____

Step #3: _____

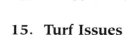
15. Turf Issues

You have just hired a temporary employee. She's essentially new to the business but has had a very brief experience in your field several years ago. She has been on the job for a month and appears to be trying to learn as much as she can, as fast as she can. You hear one of your employees, who has worked with you for five years, continuously "brow beat" her for doing stupid things. To the temporary employee, you might say:

Step #1: This is a new and challenging business for someone who has not had a lot of experience.

Step #2: May I tell you something?

Step #3: I like the way you are persevering and moving forward learning everything with all the comments passed your way.

Step #1: _____

Step #2: _____

Step #3: _____

To the employee, you might say:

Step #1: You are the best employee I have because you know this business inside and out.

Step #2: May I ask you something?

Step #3: Would you learn a new task very quickly if I was always on your back and making snide remarks? Be the model. Show the temp how to do it right!

Step #1: _____

Step #2: _____

Step #3: _____

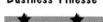

16. Working Overtime

An employee is talking to you about working so much overtime. She tells you that this is hard on her family. You say:

Step #1: Thank you for having the courage to confide in me.

Step #2: May I ask you something?

Step #3: How would you suggest we become more productive to reduce our overtime?

OR

Step #1: Thanks for coming to me with this situation.

Step #2: May I tell you something?

Step #3: This is the way the department has always operated and I'm open to suggestions for changing it.

Your language:

Step #1: _____

Step #2: _____

Step #3: _____

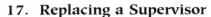

17.　Replacing a Supervisor

You have had to remove a supervisor from a specific location and replace her with a new supervisor. You want to help the new supervisor make the transition as smoothly as possible and have something challenging to say to the other employees regarding the change. At the staff meeting, you begin with:

Step #1:　Each of you was hired for your ability to make things happen, to keep things moving and to serve our customers.

Step #2:　May I share something with you?

Step #3:　We have hired Sally Go For It to head up this section because, like you, she's eager and willing to go for more.

OR

Step #1:　You know when things are going well for this section and when they aren't.

Step #2:　May I tell you something?

Step #3:　If you are ready to play a bigger game, Sally Go For It is the person to have on your team.

Your language:

Step #1: _____

Step #2: _____

Step #3: _____

★ ★ ★ ★ ★ ★ ★ ★

18. Personal Hygiene Problems

One of your employees seems to have a personal hygiene problem. You have also received some complaints from your other employees. You decide to talk with the employee.

Step #1: You are someone who does not deviate from our dress code.

Step #2: May I share something with you?

Step #3: I have noticed and am concerned about your personal hygiene.

OR

Step #1: You have always been a team member and a leader on the team.

Step #2: May I ask you something?

Step #3: Is personal hygiene a priority with you?

Your language:

Step #1: _____

Step #2: _____

Step #3: _____

19. Gossiping

You hear one of your employees gossiping about other employees in your department. You notice some tension within the department and decide to put a stop to the gossiping. You meet with the employee and say:

Step #1: You produce a lot of work during the work day.

Step #2: May I ask you something?

Step #3: How do you produce so much work and still have time to gossip?

OR

Step #1: You are a valued employee and I depend on you.

Step #2: May I tell you something?

Step #3: Other members of our group look to you as the model of workplace behavior. What can you do to set a higher standard around workplace gossip and productivity?

Your language:

Step #1: _____

Step #2: _____

Step #3: _____

20. Employee Performance Review

One of your employees is hesitant about scheduling their annual performance review with you. He has even gone so far as to brag to you that he never had a performance review for the last five years with the previous manager. You say:

Step #1: Wow! Five years without a performance review. That is a long time.

Step #2: May I tell you something?

Step #3: An annual performance review is critical for your professional development, for any promotions and for your career future.

OR

Step #1: You're right, it has been five years since your last performance review.

Step #2: May I ask you something?

Step #3: If you don't know what I think, how will you know if you are going in the right direction? How can you afford not to know what I think?

★　★　★　★　★　★　★　★

Your language:

Step #1: _____

Step #2: _____

Step #3: _____

21. Employee Performance Review, Part 2

As the manager, you have been "tardy" in completing the performance reviews for your staff. One of them has complained to you about not having his done. You respond:

Step #1: You're right to take the initiative to be fully responsible for obtaining your feedback.

Step #2: May I tell you something?

Step #3: I have been slow and it's people like you who keep me on my toes and I appreciate that.

OR

Step #3: I appreciate you taking the responsibility for scheduling this.

OR

Step #1: You're right. I have not been fully responsible for keeping you informed.

Step #2: May I tell you something?

Step #3: You are someone who will go far because you care about yourself and your future.

Your language:

Step #1: _____

Step #2: _____

Step #3: _____

22. Employee Problems

One of your employees, Joe, is blaming another employee in your department for a problem or mistake. You say to Joe:

Step #1: You have the longest safety record in this company.

Step #2: May I tell you something?

Step #3: Blaming others doesn't give you the opportunity to learn for yourself.

OR

Step #1: You are the senior staff person and people look to you as their model.

Step #2: May I ask you something?

Step #3: Do you want to solve this by learning from it or do you want to argue about who is right?

Your language:

Step #1: _____

Step #2: _____

Step #3: _____

23. Turf Issues, Part 2

You have asked one of your employees to do something and she replies that "it's not my job." You respond:

Step #1: You're right, officially it's not your job.

Step #2: May I tell you something?

Step #3: When it comes to an internal or external customer, it's always your job. It's called going the extra mile. Now tell me what you are going to do to change.

OR

Step #1:   You are right, it's not your job.

Step #2: May I tell you something?

Step #3: When you say it's not your job, you are limiting your growth personally and professionally.

Step #1: _____

Step #2: _____

Step #3: _____

24. Giving an Employee a New Assignment

You and an employee are meeting about a project that you want to give her. You are sure she will be excited about taking this project on. When you tell her, she looks away and doesn't say a word. You say:

Step #1: You're looking away and not saying a word.

Step #2: May I tell you something?

Step #3: I thought you would be excited.

OR

Step #1: You are not responding.

Step #2: May I ask you something?

Step #3: What do I need to know from you about this project?

Your language:

Step #1: _____

Step #2: _____

Step #3: _____

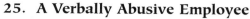

25. A Verbally Abusive Employee

You have a particularly verbally abusive employee who you are not able to terminate for various reasons. You hate to have any sort of interaction with this person so you choose to handle him this way:

Step #1: You were hired for a reason and you appear to be doing your job.

Step #2: May I tell you something?

Step #3: From this point on, if you have anything to say to me, please do it in writing. I'd rather not have a face-to-face conversation with you.

OR

Step #1: You are a tough cookie to deal with.

Step #2: Let me tell you something.

Step #3: I have a difficult time dealing face-to-face with you. Please put everything in writing to me from this point on.

Your language:

Step #1: _____

Step #2: _____

Step #3: _____

26. Employee Takes More Authority Than Approved of

One of your long-time, valued assistants has approved a Purchase Order for a vendor for an amount that exceeds her approval limit.

Step #1: Rose, you keep this office moving.

Step #2: May I tell you something?

Step #3: You exceeded your approval limit with that P.O.

OR

Step #1: Jim, you are someone who gets things done around here.

Step #2: May I tell you something?

Step #3: A P.O. over $500 requires my approval and signature. Please honor this policy in the future.

Your language:

Step #1: _____

Step #2: _____

Step #3: _____

27. Employee is Not Fulfilling Job Responsibilities

Your assistant is not carrying out her responsibilities on the job, especially when it comes to XYZ project that you both are working on. You have casually mentioned this to her but it hasn't seemed to work. Today you have decided to say something more formal.

Step #1: You are someone who people feel comfortable talking to.

Step #2: May I share something with you?

Step #3: You have not followed up on the XYZ project and I am wondering what's happening with you. This is not like you.

Be careful to listen for the truth here. Whatever she says, don't go along with it unless you can stand behind it 100%. If she cries, let her. Don't try to help her. Let her help herself.

OR

Step #1: You are one of my top performers.

Step #2: May I tell you something?

Step #3: Something is going on with you. I don't know what it is and I'm not even sure I can help you. If you want to tell me, I'm willing to listen.

Your language:

Step #1: _____

Step #2: _____

Step #3: _____

28. Peer Harassment

One of your peers, a manager in the department next to yours has been coming into your office and telling you stories about his escapades with his girlfriend the night before. You pretend to be doing other things or you have told him you are busy but he just keeps talking. Today, when he begins to recount his stories, you say:

Step #1: You are a good story teller.

Step #2: May I tell you something?

Step #3: If you say one more word about your date, I will file a complaint against you.

OR

Step #1: You enjoy telling a story.

Step #2: May I tell you something?

Step #3: I am not impressed with your stories and, in fact, I am offended by them. Please stop them immediately or I will take action.

Your language:

Step #1: _____

Step #2: _____

Step #3: _____

Section 2: Dealing With the Boss

1. The Boss is Indecisive

You are meeting with your boss to review a new way of doing things in your department and to make a decision. You want to be certain that you know what to do at the end of the meeting. However, your boss says that you need to wait awhile before you change anything.

Step #1: You are right. There's no rush to implement this idea.

Step #2: May I ask you something?

Step #3: Do you think it would be helpful to increase our bottom line by next quarter?

OR

Step #1: You are right, we can probably afford to wait on this.

Step: #2: May I tell you something?

Step #3: This will reduce overtime by 5%.

Your language:

Step #1: _____

Step #2: _____

Step #3: _____

2. A New Assignment You Are Unsure of

Your boss has just told you to do something you have never done before. She did not give you any information about how to do it and she didn't give you any time to ask questions. You feel left hanging in the wind and concerned that you may not do the job right and therefore look bad in her eyes. You say to her:

Step #1: Thank you for your confidence in me.

Step #2: I need to tell you one thing.

Step #3: I don't know how to do what you have asked me to do. Who can I check with for further information?

OR

Step #1: Thank you for asking me to take on this project.

Step #2: May I tell you something?

Step #3: I don't know where to begin and I need some help in getting started. Who do you suggest I begin with?

Your language:

Step #1: _____

Step #2: _____

Step #3: _____

3. An Inconsistent Boss

Your boss called you five minutes ago and told you what a great job you are doing managing the flow and your staff. He just called you two seconds ago and now tells you that you are doing a terrible job and you are definitely not management material. After the first call, you said, "Thank you!" After the second call, you say:

Step #1: You have every right to give me your opinion.

Step #2: May I ask you something?

Step #3: Why have you changed your mind about my performance in the last five minutes?

OR

Step #1: Wow! You really do have a strong opinion about me.

Step #2: May I tell you something?

Step #3: I work best with someone who focuses on my strengths and challenges me to improve my performance.

Your language:

Step #1: _____

Step #2: _____

Step #3: _____

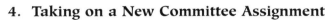

4. Taking on a New Committee Assignment

You have heard about an ad hoc committee that your boss is putting together. You want to be on this committee because the project is one that you are very interested in pursuing. You approach the boss and say:

Step #1: You are someone who has guided my growth and development in the company.

Step #2: May I ask you something?

Step #3: Would you be willing to include me on the ad hoc committee?

OR

Step #1: It took someone like you to take action on this project.

Step #2: May I tell you something?

Step #3: This project is of particular interest to me and I would like to be included on the committee.

Your language:

Step #1: _____

Step #2: _____

Step #3: _____

5. Your Boss is Taking You for Granted

Your boss seems to be taking you for granted by not giving you any challenging projects. You truly enjoy working for this man. You have always learned a lot from him but lately, you feel like he isn't talking to you as much as he used to and you don't feel like he really appreciates you. You say to him:

Step #1: It has been a pleasure and a real honor to work with you these past eight years.

Step #2: May I ask you something?

Step #3: Am I as valuable to you as I was eight years ago?

OR

Step #1: I have enjoyed learning from you and growing within the department.

Step #2: May I tell you something?

Step #3: I would like to take on more challenging projects that we design together and you feel comfortable giving to me.

Your language:

Step #1: _____

Step #2: _____

Step #3: _____

6. Bogged Down With Projects

Your boss is always asking you to take on one more task. You are working overtime as it is and can barely see the light of day. She has just come into your office and asked you to handle the new XYZ project. You respond:

Step #1: Thank you for having confidence in me.

Step #2: May I ask you something?

Step #3: Which one do you want me to give priority to, the ABC project, the MNO project or this one?

OR

Step #1: Thanks for recognizing my skills.

Step #2: May I tell you something?

Step #3: I am completely bogged down with the other two projects. Is this the time for me to start this or would you rather we schedule it in later?

Your language:

Step #1: _____

Step #2: _____

Step #3: _____

7. The Employee Dress Code, Part 2

Your boss mentions to you that one of your employees isn't adhering to the dress code. You've noticed it, too, but haven't said anything about it.

Step #1: You are right. Joe is not following the company dress code.

Step #2: May I tell you something?

Step #3: I noticed it, too, but didn't say anything and I'm willing to fix that this morning.

OR

Step #1: You are right. She's not adhering to our guidelines.

Step #2: May I ask you something?

Step #3: How would you handle this with Jane?

Your language:

Step #1: _____

Step #2: _____

Step #3: _____

8. Your Performance Review

It's performance review time for you and you're sitting in your boss's office. She says: "Your turnover is the highest in the company. People are beginning to wonder what is wrong. What's the problem here?"

Step #1: You are right. Turnover is high in my department.

Step #2: Do you want to know why?

Step #3: I'm not willing to go down to the lowest common denominator when it comes to my people. I want everyone on the same game plan and I'm willing to challenge them, work with them and cheer them on. And if they don't get it, I'm willing to let them go. It sends a poor message to the entire team when one person isn't pulling his weight.

OR

Step #1: You are right. We do have the highest turnover.

Step #2: May I tell you why?

Step #3: We have a team and every member is doing 110%. If someone isn't, they won't be willing to stay around too long to take the heat.

Your language:

Step #1: _____

Step #2: _____

Step #3: _____

9. Job Security

You have heard rumors about the future of your job and your department within the company. Rumor says that your department may be eliminated. You make an appointment to see your boss.

Step #1: Joe, I have always enjoyed working with you.

Step #2: May I ask you something?

Step #3: What do you see as the next step in my career development?

OR

Step #1: Jane, thanks for having the open door policy.

Step #2: May I tell you something?

Step #3: With the re-alignment of the company, I don't see how my present position and even my department will be viable. Tell me your thoughts.

Your language:

Step #1: _____

Step #2: _____

Step #3: _____

10. Committee Assignment, Part 2

Your boss has asked you to serve on a committee at work. You are not really a committee type person, BUT you don't want to disappoint your boss and you would like to use it to gain better visibility within the organization.

Step #1: Thank you for asking me to serve on this committee.

Step #2: May I tell you something?

Step #3: I definitely want to serve you. Here's my problem. I am not great on details, so would I be doing you a disservice if I served?

OR

Step #1: Thank you for considering me as a committee member.

Step #2: May I tell you something?

Step #3: What I am good at is . . . . Is it possible for me to serve on the committee in this capacity?

Your language:

Step #1: _____

Step #2: _____

Step #3: _____

11. Job Burn-out

Your boss appears to be physically and emotionally exhausted. He seems to be snapping at everyone yet not accomplishing anything. Here's what you say:

Step #1: Irv, you have always been the leader and shown us the way.

Step #2: May I tell you something?

Step #3: I really need you to support me with this new project. I want you to agree with a, b, and c as I bring them up. You don't have to say anything else but support me 100% on these three items. Are you willing to do that?

OR

Step #1: You look like the dog ate your last candy bar.

Step #2: May I tell you something?

Step #3: I need you today at the meeting with the area supervisors. If you're behind me, they won't tell me "no."

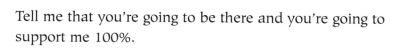

Tell me that you're going to be there and you're going to support me 100%.

Your language:

Step #1: _____

Step #2: _____

Step #3: _____

12. Requesting What You Need From Your Boss

You have sent a proposal to your boss about fully automating (computerizing) your department. You are in her office now and the first words out of her mouth regarding your proposal are: "Your people work hard for you. The workload is growing but all you need to do is hire another person." You respond with:

Step #1: You are right. We could hire another person.

Step #2: May I tell you something?

Step #3: Over the next 12 months, the cost of computerizing our department would save us $xxx while hiring a new person would cost us $xxx.

OR

Step #1: You are right. The staff work extremely hard.

Step #2: May I share something with you?

Step #3: Our productivity would increase by X% as indicated in the proposal and our cost per employee would be reduced. At the same time, I have polled the staff and there is no one who is resistant to the idea.

Your language:

Step #1: _____

Step #2: _____

Step #3: _____

13. The Verbally Abusive Boss

Your boss is yelling at you to come to his office and he doesn't sound happy. You have no idea what this is all about. When you walk in, he's still yelling and when there is a pause, you say:

Step #1: You are really angry about something.

Step #2: May I tell you something?

Step #3: I don't feel good about this verbal attack and I really would like to walk out of here.

OR

Step #1: You are really upset.

Step #2: May I tell you something?

Step #3: I want to work with you in a way that leaves both of us feeling empowered and respectful of each other.

OR

Step #1: You are really hurting.

Step #2: May I tell you something?

Step #3: I don't feel safe in giving you feedback right now.

Your language:

Step #1: _____

Step #2: _____

Step #3: _____

14. The Boss is Retiring

You are at the party and feel a little uncomfortable because he has been your mentor and friend and you hate to see him go. You don't want to lose track of him so you say,

Step #1: You have been an inspiration to me and to many others here.

Step #2: May I tell you something?

Step #3: I would still like to have our Monday meetings via telephone, if that's all right with you. I'll call you Monday at 10 to set up a convenient time for both of us.

OR

Step #1: You have been the backbone of this department.

Step #2: May I ask you something?

Step #3: May I call you from time to time for your opinion?

Your language:

Step #1: _____

Step #2: _____

Step #3: _____

Section 3: Dealing With External Clients

1. A Call From a Client at an Inconvenient Time of Day

For those of us who take all kinds of calls during the day, here's the solution to maintaining control over your time. With clients, keep in mind that they expect you to run your department as a business, just as they run their business. It's your responsibility to yourself, your clients and your work that you manage your actions and have your business day flow smoothly.

If a client calls asking for information and it is inconvenient, say:

Step #1: You're right, I do have the information about that project.

Step #2: May I tell you something?

Step #3: I am right in the middle of a meeting. May I call you back within the hour?

OR

Step #1: You're right. I am the one to help you with that.

Step #2: May I ask you something?

Step #3: May I get back to you at 8 am tomorrow?

Your language:

Step #1: _____

Step #2: _____

Step #3: _____

2. A Personal Call During the Work Day

Friends, who are also clients, always have a tendency to call during the work day to talk about "friend stuff." You love them and you want to continue serving them but you also want to stay focused on your business. When personal calls from clients get out of hand, or even before this time, say:

Step #1: I'm glad you called and I want to talk to you about that situation.

Step #2: May I tell you something?

Step #3: I'm preparing my presentation for the staff meeting and I don't want to lose my focus. Would you be willing to talk about this tonight? May I call you at home?

OR

Step #1: Joe, I love to hear from you.

Step #2: May I tell you something?

Step #3: I have a bid to get out by 5 pm. May I call you back at 5:30 pm?

Your language:

Step #1: _____

Step #2: _____

Step #3: _____

3. Re-educating a Client About Your New Position

Many of us change jobs or job descriptions, and you need to have an effective way to let your clients know about this move. This is particularly important if you have dealt with clients on a one-to-one basis. (It's critical for clients to know exactly what you do now and who might be working with them in the future.) If a client calls you and says she has heard that there have been some changes in your department, say:

Step #1: You are right, I do have a new title.

Step #2: May I tell you something?

Step #3: This promotion means that I will be taking on new customer service responsibilities as well as an increase in the number of customers I deal with.

OR

Step #1: You are right. I won't be handling your account in the future.

Step #2: May I tell you something?

Step #3: Sara Smith will be your account representative and will be calling you within the next two weeks to come by and visit with you.

Your language:

Step #1: _____

Step #2: _____

Step #3: _____

4. Asking the Client to Reconsider

Many times the client thinks they know what they want and they are certain about it. However, if you feel strongly about your offer, ask them to reconsider.

Step #1: You are right to be concerned about the changes in the contract.

Step #2: May I share something with you?

Step #3: These changes will reduce your monthly fee by 12%.

OR

Step #1: You are right to take the time to talk to your boss about this.

Step #2: May I tell you something?

Step #3: This is so important that I request that you talk with your boss today and re-schedule our meeting for tomorrow morning.

Your language:

Step #1: _____

Step #2: _____

Step #3: _____

5. To Obtain a Face to Face Meeting With a Client

You know you could help them with their service problems but you just can't seem to pin the decision-maker down for a meeting, and you don't like to talk on the phone. You are getting impatient with this client. Perhaps you will just let them solve their own problems. You finally have the decision-maker on the phone and want to set up a meeting. She says she is just too busy right now. Next month would be better. You say:

Step #1: You really are a busy person, especially in this economy.

Step #2: May I ask you something?

Step #3: Are you ready for us to get together and work this thing out in person or do you really want it to linger for another month?

OR

Step #1: You are too busy to keep putting out fires.

Step #2: May I tell you something?

Step #3: I'm willing to meet with you anytime within the next two weeks and get the customer service issues solved.

Your language:

Step #1: _____

Step #2: _____

Step #3: _____

6. Handling a Social Request from A Client

You have just been asked out to dinner by your client, of the opposite sex, and there is no business reason given for the dinner. You feel very uncomfortable with this invitation. You sense there is more to this than a simple dinner.

Step #1: It's always a pleasure to meet with you.

Step #2: May I share something with you?

Step #3: I have a policy not to attend social events with my clients.

OR

Step #1: You are very kind.

Step #2: May I tell you something?

Step #3: I don't feel comfortable with this invitation. If there's a business reason, let's meet during working hours.

★ ★ ★ ★ ★ ★ ★ ★

Your language:

Step #1: _____

Step #2: _____

Step #3: _____

7. Your Client Tries to Manipulate a Contract

During a contract negotiation, a client has asked you to complete a project for them sooner than you and your company feels comfortable doing. The client says that if you don't do it in their time frame, they will give the contract to XYZ Corporation down the street who will.

Step #1: You're right, you do need to work with a company who will provide you the services you need when you need them.

Step #2: May I share something with you?

Step #3: XYZ Corporation will not be able to complete the job any sooner than we can.

OR

Step #1: You are right to work with a company that can handle your needs.

Step #2: May I tell you something?

Step #3: We will only agree to a contract that provides an adequate time frame for us to build what you need and to the specifications that you give us. If we reduce that time frame, we would not be able to guarantee our work.

Your language:

Step #1: _____

Step #2: _____

Step #3: _____

8. Customer Complaints

One of your customers calls and leaves two very nasty voice mail messages saying that one of your employees is not handling things in accordance with your contract and if you don't fix it, he'll take his business elsewhere. Your investigation shows that your employee did everything according to the contract and has kept telephone notes documenting her conversation with the customer's employee. You have decided to call your customer and ask permission to talk with his employee which he gives you. You call the customer's employee and say,

Step #1: You have worked well with our company and customer service department for a long time.

Step #2: May I ask you something?

Step #3: What is the problem between you and Charlene?

OR

Step #1: My customer service people have nothing but great things to say about you.

Step #2: May I tell you something?

Step #3: I was surprised to hear what you told your boss about Charlene.

He might then say, "Well, we didn't get our shipment on time and you are the shippers."

You respond with Business Finesse:

Step #1: You are right. We are the shippers.

Step #2: May I ask you something?

Step #3: Didn't you tell customer service to ship on Thursday instead of Wednesday?

He says, "Well, I thought I said Wednesday."

Step #1: You probably thought you said Wednesday.

Step #2: May I tell you something?

Step #3: Our telephone log shows that you called back and changed it to Thursday.

Your language:

Step #1: _____

Step #2: _____

Step #3: _____

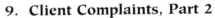

9. Client Complaints, Part 2

You get a call from one of your clients complaining about the service one of your employees gave them. This is not a customer who usually complains. Your first words are:

Step #1: You have every right to expect great service from our company and our employees.

Step #2: May I ask you something?

Step #3: Will you tell me exactly what happened, when it happened and how it impacted your business?

OR

Step #1: You have every right to be concerned and to complain.

Step #2: Will you tell me something?

Step #3: How do you want me to handle this with this particular employee?

Your language:

Step #1: _____

Step #2: _____

Step #3: _____

Think about this:

When you use scripts to practice the language you need to get exactly what you want, you will get a lot more. An actor or actress doesn't play the Academy award winning role without using a script. Why should you go through your workday without a script? Do you want to win? Use the scripts!

Part 3

Chapter 9

Why Use Business Finesse -- The Pros and The Cons

"Do or do not. There is no try."
Yoda

In Part III, I will use the word, client, quite frequently. In doing so, keep in mind that whenever I use the word "client," I am talking about your internal clients (the boss, your staff, co-workers) and your external clients (your customers).

Why is this skill, Business Finesse, important to use?

You may be under the false impression that just saying the first thing off the top of your head is communicating. Actually, it is a waste of everyone's time and, in many cases, it makes people very defensive. So defensive, in fact, that they put their shields up and you know what happens when shields go up! Review Chapter 3.

Your clients will respond to you the way you respond to them. If you say the same thing you have always said, you will get the same reaction from them that you always have. Why should it be different? Nothing else has changed. However, when you change, they will have to change how they respond to you. It will be very difficult for them to respond the same way to you when you are using this skill, Business Finesse. In fact, it's impossible!

If you know what to say, how to say it and when to say it, you'll create a lot more with your clients. When you master this three step process, communication occurs at the spiritual level rather than the emotional level. When this happens, effective communication takes place and you build long-term relationships, are more productive and more profitable.

★   ★   ★   ★   ★   ★   ★   ★

What is the consequence of not using Business Finesse?

In most cases, if you say the thing that first comes to your mind in any communication process, you'll connect at the mind or emotional level with the other person. When you connect at the mind level, you engage the ego. When you engage the ego, you can be guaranteed of feeling upset, irrational, or very emotional. When you engage the ego, that usually moves the conversation way off base so you and your client are not even focusing on what is important but what the ego thinks is important. As you become more ego involved, you lose credibility with your clients. They don't know what set you off or got you off the track and they really don't care. They completely miss that they are communicating at the emotional level and so are you. They can only see you. It certainly has nothing to do with them-- so they think. From their perspective, you are kind of weird. When the client thinks you are kind of weird, you have lost the war, not just the battle. You may think you have only lost the battle. Hide and watch.

By not using the skill of Business Finesse, you failed to keep your eye on what you really wanted. You failed to sustain your client relationships, your productivity and your profitability. Even if the alligators are snapping at your rear-end, keep your focus on what you really want. Drain the swamp. Forget about the emotional connection--the alligators.

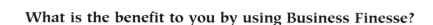

What is the benefit to you by using Business Finesse?

When you use the skill of Business Finesse, you have better and more long-term relationships with your clients. You experience more peace, focus, balance and energy because you are connecting at the heart level. You don't have to wage a war with the ego. You are living in a time of peace and prosperity with your clients.

When you use the skill of Business Finesse, you are more productive. You save time, you save giving your clients the third degree and you save effort. When you are highly productive, you experience a sense of forward movement, momentum and passion because you know how to use your time and your client's time effectively.

When you use the skill of Business Finesse, you are more profitable. It means that you no longer have to work harder for the client. You are now working in conjunction with the client. You and the client are standing shoulder-to-shoulder and moving forward. You no longer have to carry the client down the yellow-brick road. They are walking right by your side. You experience joy. And when you feel good, you have more creative and innovative ideas for your clients, as you see what's possible for them.

How do you know if you are not using Business Finesse?

Clue #1. You are having a lot of emotional reactions. You are tired, irritable, anxious and concerned about what's going to happen.

Clue #2: You are asking your clients a lot of questions but you never seem to get the right answer or one that makes sense.

Clue #3: You are wearing yourself out by chasing after your clients.

Clue #4: Your clients seem to be very evasive and seem to be enjoying it.

Clue #5: You have long discussions with your clients that seem to go nowhere.

Clue #6: Your clients cancel appointments with you.

Clue #7: Your clients repeat themselves or ramble.

Clue #8: Your clients blame you for current problems they are having.

Clue #9: You no longer have easy access to your clients and you feel pretty rejected.

Clue #10: You don't know what to do next with your clients.

What can you expect to see happen to your clients when you use Business Finesse?

They will relax because you have connected with them at the heart level. You have not engaged the ego so there is no emotional baggage with which to deal. Once they relax with

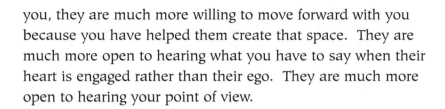
you, they are much more willing to move forward with you because you have helped them create that space. They are much more open to hearing what you have to say when their heart is engaged rather than their ego. They are much more open to hearing your point of view.

They will be surprised that you have connected with them on the heart level. The surprise will show in their face. In fact, you might even be able to see and hear as they take off their suit of armor and extend a hand in camaraderie to you.

They will begin to talk with you rather than at you because you are communicating at the heart level. They no longer have to defend themselves against ego attack, they can be a team with you because you made them right, honored their time and boundaries and told them the truth.

They will tell you more from their heart and take more risks with you because you have built a relationship. You'll see more of the results you really want for them as well as for you. And they'll help you create them.

Think about this:

When you use the skill of Business Finesse, your internal and external clients will notice a change in you. And because you have changed, they will change.

Part 3

Chapter 10

Reviewing The Process

"Nobody can help being born common, but ain't nobody got to remain ordinary."

Satchel Paige

1. **What worked?** List the parts of this process that worked for you. Then ask yourself why they worked?

_____

_____

_____

_____

_____

_____

_____

_____

_____

_____

_____

Now ask yourself why the other parts didn't? Did you use the three steps? Did you use the language? What happened? What stopped you from communicating at the spiritual level? Tell the truth here. This is an opportunity to explode any belief systems that no longer work for you but may be holding you back from communicating effectively.

What Didn't Work   Why?

_____   _____

_____   _____

_____   _____

_____   _____

_____   _____

_____   _____

_____   _____

_____   _____

_____   _____

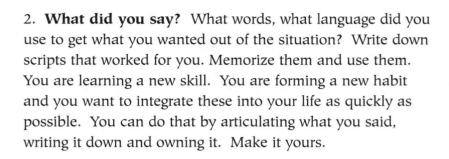

2. **What did you say?** What words, what language did you use to get what you wanted out of the situation? Write down scripts that worked for you. Memorize them and use them. You are learning a new skill. You are forming a new habit and you want to integrate these into your life as quickly as possible. You can do that by articulating what you said, writing it down and owning it. Make it yours.

List the situation:

Step #1:

Step #2:

Step #3:

3. **Did the other person react or respond to you?**
People are trained to communicate at the emotional level. You want to become aware of this as you communicate with people because when you can observe it, you can then make a mental note to stay at the spiritual level rather than getting seduced back down to the emotional level.

Emotional Communication = head to head communication.

Spiritual Communication = heart to heart communication.

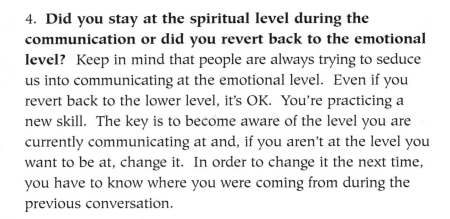

4. Did you stay at the spiritual level during the communication or did you revert back to the emotional level? Keep in mind that people are always trying to seduce us into communicating at the emotional level. Even if you revert back to the lower level, it's OK. You're practicing a new skill. The key is to become aware of the level you are currently communicating at and, if you aren't at the level you want to be at, change it. In order to change it the next time, you have to know where you were coming from during the previous conversation.

5. During your last "sticky" communication, what was different about you? How did you do things/say things differently? How did you change from the time before? You want to continue to articulate how you have changed. When you can articulate how you havechanged, you can then see what's different about you and how you are now coming from a different place when you communicate. Go back to the sticky situation and see the new part of you that was created when you used Business Finesse. List your new strengths.

What are your Inner Strengths?
1.
2.
3.
4.
5.

★ ★ ★ ★ ★ ★ ★ ★

What are your Professional Strengths?

1.

2.

3.

4.

5.

It's a clean, stronger part. It's the truth about you. You always do the best you can and each sticky situation is a growth opportunity for you.

6. **How did the other person respond to the "different" you?** What was different about him or her? It's funny how when we change, others seems to change, too. Keep in mind that it is futile to try to change others. However, when we change, the whole dynamic of the relationship changes and you will see that they have changed, too.

7. **What did you discover about yourself in dealing with this particular sticky situation?** Most of the time we give so much power to things "outside" ourselves but the truth is that we are the strong ones. When you use Business Finesse, you see how well you can handle these sticky situations. You see that it's about how you act and what you say rather than it being about them.

8. **What did you discover about them?** If you change how you communicate, they will change how they communicate, too. It's human nature. They can't continue to come from the emotional level when you are coming from the spiritual level. They will change.

★143★

9. **Who are you now because you are using the skill of Business Finesse?** Use the language: "Now I am someone who. . . ." Perhaps you are now someone who can communicate on a different level. Or you are someone who can see the strengths in everyone regardless of the level of communication they are coming from. You may be someone who can now see more about what you want. You are experiencing and coming to see more parts of you so you can see just how powerful, assertive and focused you really are. When you can see who you are, you can see better who everyone else is, too.

I am someone who _____

_____.

10. **What things, if any, will you do differently in the future?** As you practice this skill, you are forming a new habit, a new way of being. You begin to see who you used to be and who you are now and where you are going. You are the master of your ship, of your soul. You can always choose where to go, who to be and how to be. You are really the only one who can do that. The other person can't do it for you. It's up to you. You get to choose.

When you change where you come from, you discover something new about yourself and about others. It's refreshing, it's freeing, it's miraculous and it keeps you from getting stuck in a rut.

Think about this:

Are you practicing the three-steps of Business Finesse?
Can you articulate who you now are because
you use this skill?
Can you detect when you are communicating
at the emotional rather than spiritual level?
Can you make people right even if they
are wrong?

Part 3
Chapter 11
Conclusion

"We cannot be a source of strength unless we nurture our own strength."

M. Scott Peck

If you say what you've always said, you'll get what you've always gotten. If you use the same words you've always used, you'll get the same response or reaction that you've always gotten. Is that OK with you? I hope not.

Who has never been at a loss for words. When we are at a loss for words, we usually turn our anger inward on ourselves, and thereby experience isolation and loneliness. We don't understand what happens to us in business encounters because of our inability to ask for exactly what we want or to tell the truth. Communicating what we really want is difficult. We usually hold back some part of the communication or say something to make the other person feel better, or use vague statements because we are unsure of what we want. Fully responsible business communicators are aware of what they say, how they say it and how they are heard.

Your internal and external clients want to be around you and do business with you. What they need from you is to be communicated with at the spiritual level. You may be conditioned to react at the emotional level to give your ideas or fix things but unless you connect at the heart level, your employees, boss or customers won't hear what you have to say or see what you are trying to do. When you use the skill of Business Finesse, you connect with them at the heart level and when that happens, you can eliminate the barriers between you to make the heart to heart connection every single time you communicate. By doing this, you communicate a lot more--and you communicate more effectively.

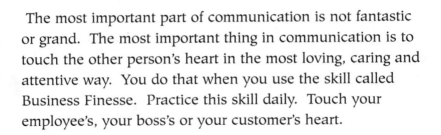
The most important part of communication is not fantastic or grand. The most important thing in communication is to touch the other person's heart in the most loving, caring and attentive way. You do that when you use the skill called Business Finesse. Practice this skill daily. Touch your employee's, your boss's or your customer's heart.

What I want for you today is to develop a foundation in order to begin trusting yourself and your problem-solving skills because now you know the process of Business Finesse and you have practiced it. Make a habit of it.

Here's a way to do that. Examine your ability to communicate effectively on a daily basis. Yes, that's right-- daily! Ask yourself these questions:

1. What exactly do I want out of this situation or from this person?

2. What is the truth about why I want it? (If you have to justify or gather evidence, it is not your truth.)

3. Am I willing to make this person right even though they may be absolutely wrong?

4. Am I willing to wait for their full attention before giving my ideas or opinions or advice?

5. Am I willing to say it all, mindful of the consequences, and regardless of the consequences?

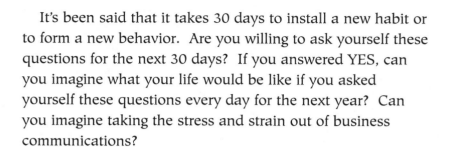

It's been said that it takes 30 days to install a new habit or to form a new behavior. Are you willing to ask yourself these questions for the next 30 days? If you answered YES, can you imagine what your life would be like if you asked yourself these questions every day for the next year? Can you imagine taking the stress and strain out of business communications?

Effective communicators ask themselves these questions daily and they move forward towards making a habit out of using Business Finesse and communicating effectively.

Business Finesse is a way of changing where you come from with your employee, your boss and your customers. Changing your perspective of where you come from is not about doing a lot of work. It is simply a two degree shift in your thinking in order to come from a new place; in order to change the dynamic of how you relate to your internal and external clients; in order for you to have much, much better employee, boss and customer relationships, be more productive and more profitable.

Appendix

Things that Make Me Smile When I Do Them By Myself	Things That Make Me Smile When I Do Them With One Other Person	Things That Make Me Smile When I Do Them With A Group
1	1.	1.
2.	2.	2.
3.	3.	3.
4	4.	4.
5.	5.	5.
6.	6.	6.
7.	7.	7.
8.	8.	8.
9.	9.	9.
10.	10.	10.
11.	11.	11.
12.	12.	12.
13.	13.	13.
14.	14.	14.
15.	15.	15.
16.	16.	16.
17.	17.	17.
18.	18.	18.
19.	19.	19.
20.	20.	20.
21.	21.	21.
22.	22.	22.
23.	23.	23.
24.	24.	24.
25.	25.	25.

Situation:

Step #1:

Step #2:

Step #3:

Situation:

Step #1:

Step #2:

Step #3:

Bibliography

Allen, James, *As a Man Thinketh*, Grossett & Dunlap, 1959.

Breathnach, Sara Ban, *Simple Abundance*, Warner Books, 1995.

Bridges, William, *Transitions*, Addison-Wesley, 1980.

Butterworth, Eric, *Spiritual Economics*, Unity Books, 1983.

Gawain, Shakti, *Creative Visualization*, New World Library, 1978.

Gerber, Michael E., *The E Myth Revisited*, HarperBusiness, 1995.

Keyes, Ken, *How to Enjoy Your Life in Spite of It All*, Living Love Publications, 1980.

Mandino, Og, *The Greatest Miracle in the World*, Bonanza Books, 1968.

Peters, Tom, *The Pursuit of WOW!*, Vintage Books, 1994.

Roman, Sanaya, *Personal Power Through Awareness* , H. J. Kramer, 1986.

Roman, Sanaya, *Spiritual Growth*, H. J. Kramer, 1989.

Shanklin, Imelda, *What Are You?*, Unity Books, 1995.

Sinetar, Marsha, *Developing a 21st-Century Mind*, Ballantine Books, 1991.

von Oech, Roger, *A Whack on the Side of the Head*, Warner Books, 1983.

Whitfield, Charles, *Healing the Child Within*, Health Communications, 1987.

Williamson, Marianne, *A Return to Love*, HarperCollins, 1992.

Index

Contact Information

Linda Talley is a popular keynote speaker at conventions and corporations on communication strategies, personal leadership and performance. If you would like more information about other products and services offered by Linda Talley and Leadership University, contact:

Linda Talley
P.O. Box 22414
Houston, Texas 77227-2414
713-960-1067
FAX 713-960-1131
email: LTCOACH@aol.com
http://www.lindatalley.com